THE JAMES EARL SMITH STORY

A Personal Account of Life, Family, and War

JON STROUD

CHICAGO SPECTRUM PRESS
12305 WESTPORT RD.
LOUISVILLE, KENTUCKY 40245
502-899-1919

Printed in the U.S.A.

10 9 8 7 6 5 4 3

ISBN: 978-158374-274-7

For more information about The James Earl Smith Story or to order more copies of the book, go to:

thejamesearlsmithstory@gmail.com

World War II photos purchased from the U.S. Navy Historical Foundation and the U.S. National Archives.

This book is dedicated to my grandmother, Marion Anita Smith, the last surviving member of my family's elder generation. I want to thank my immediate family, the James E. Smith family, and the children and grandchildren of Ruth, Bill, Carl, Earl, and Nina for their support and assistance in this book's creation. I would especially like to thank those who helped me through countless personal conversations, e-mails, phone calls, interviews, and research, as well as their emotional and financial support.

Also, thanks to Michael L. Jones, Cary Stemle, and Justin Cartwright (map illustrator).

CONTENTS

Introduction

> *"A Japanese cruiser was within city blocks away of us, and we were about to be sunk," Earl said. "We were dead, but the* St. Louis *came in between us and fired." Earl took a moment as he recalled the battle, and cried.*

My grandfather, James Earl Smith, did a lot of traveling in his 90 year lifetime. During his 30 year military career, which included seeing intense combat during World War II, he figured he circled the globe at least 24 times, crossing the Atlantic Ocean almost 40 times and stopping in many countries along the way. Because of the demands of the war, Navy ships were constantly on the move; during one two year stretch, Smith and his crewmates got off the ship only once, and he went six years without seeing his family in Kentucky. He was not the only Smith who made sacrifices in the war; his two older brothers were also off fighting.

Smith was a witness to history—he was stationed in Hawaii when the Japanese Imperial Navy attacked the U.S. fleet at Pearl Harbor and he was in the Pacific for subsequent battles, some of them among the deadliest confrontations of the war.

It seems incredible, and it is. Yet, as he neared the end of his life and reflected on everything that happened over his 90 years, including everything he saw in the military, he said that family was the most important thing. "I never enjoyed anything as much than the time I had with my parents and siblings…" unless, "it was when I became a father and a family man."

James Earl Smith's journey began in Glasgow, Kentucky, on December 23, 1920. He was the fourth of five children, born at home to James William Smith and Lottie Jane Denham in an area that was extremely rural, even for a region known as being in the backwoods. To this day, family stories live on about a black bear that stayed under the small house at night and could be heard crawling out in the early morning hours.

Because his father was also named James, everyone referred to the youngest boy as Earl (although he would pick up a few other nicknames in his lifetime). Ahead of Earl in the birth order were Ruth Francis, William Paul, and Carl Thurman, with Nina (pronounced Nyna) Belle, being the baby of the family.

Chapter One

JIM W.

Like his parents before him, Earl's father Jim W. (D.O.B. March 26, 1892) was born on a farm in Smith County, Tennessee. He was also known as Will or Willy, as well as Jim W., the third oldest of eight children of John David (David) and Martha Vandelia (Vanny) Younger Smith. His siblings were Larra, Charles, Otis, Bettie, Allie, Ernest, and Carsie.

David, was born to James R. and Ruth Jones Smith of Smith County, Tennessee, and Vanny was the daughter of William and Amanda Carter Younger, born near Red Boiling Springs in Macon County, Tennessee. William Younger and his family eventually moved into the adjoining county, Smith County, located 60 miles northeast of Nashville. During the Civil War (which began in 1861), as Tennesseans, David's father, James R., was drafted in 1863, and Vanny's father, William, voluntarily enlisted to fight for the Confederate Army.

Vanny, as a young woman, is remembered as tall and thin, with long black hair and bright blue eyes. These eyes can still be seen in the family lineage today. Vanny was a cousin to Thomas Coleman "Cole" Younger, an American confederate guerilla of the Civil War, who teamed with Jesse James to form the James-Younger gang, the notorious band of fugitives who became the most well-known outlaws of their day. David and Vanny married in the late 1880s, lived on the Younger farm and began to raise a family.

Times were different then, and Jim W. lost a brother while growing up. It wasn't uncommon for children to die young during that time period and the Smith family was no exception—David and Vanny's oldest

John David and Vanny Younger Smith, circa 1930

Front row (l. to r.) Jim W., Otis
Back row (l. to r.) Carsie, Ernest, circa 1930

son Charles (Charlie) died in 1907 at 18 years old. Though some may not believe it, a story has been passed down over the years about his death.

Charlie and his younger brother Jim W. had been working in the fields all day. Near dusk as they finished up, they tried to pull two wagons up a steep hill with two horses, but because of the heavy load they had to use both horses for each wagon. While returning to the bottom of the hill for the second wagon, they were said to have seen, just under the horizon, a horse and a wagon driven by a headless man. The headless horseman rode in plain sight across the road to the other side and disappeared into the woods.

Crossing multiple family generations, with times being difficult, many bad events would occur for which families had no explanation (unlike now, when most events, such as illness-related deaths, can be explained). In effort to make sense of these events, people would then come to believe that a future event could be foretold by an unrelated prior event.

Charlie died three days after allegedly seeing the headless horseman. The death record reported sudden hemorrhagic shock, probably from the rapid onset of flu related hemorrhagic pneumonia that in just over ten years became known as the 1918 Flu pandemic. But, David and Vanny, who were quite superstitious, believed the supposed sighting of this rider, was a premonition of Charlie's death.

In 1911, when Jim W. was 19, David moved the family from the Younger farm in Smith County to Tompkinsville in Monroe County, Kentucky, just across the state line, 40 miles away.

David worked as a mail carrier in each town and owned his own mail contract in Tompkinsville. With a horse and buggy, he traveled between Tompkinsville and 30 miles north into Glasgow, Barren County, Kentucky, having to stay one night in each.

David and Vanny lived in Tompkinsville for eleven years until moving to Glasgow, where they remained until their deaths. David died in 1935 from tuberculosis at age 71. Vanny died in 1943 of related heart and stroke complications. She was 79.

Though he could not read, Jim W. worked for his father as a rural route mail carrier in Tompkinsville. He used a team of four horses and

Uncle Ode (Otis), the front passenger in a Model T car, circa 1910

Uncle Ode (front right) with friends, circa 1910

a stage coach that transported the mail (and even passengers) between towns. Jim W. carried the mail for several years, even during harsh weather that occasionally had ice hanging from the horses' bellies.

Betty Smith, Jim W.'s sister, circa 1920

Larra (Dolly) Smith, Jim W.'s sister, circa 1910

In 1920, Jim W., now with a family of his own, moved from Tompkinsville to Glasgow two years before his parents. Glasgow was slightly larger and offered better opportunities. He then changed professions and began painting houses.

Glasgow wasn't his last stop. In 1924, Jim W. moved north again, this time 100 miles, to Louisville, Kentucky, where he continued to make his living painting and doing odd jobs.

Jim W. was a slender and soft-spoken man, and, like his parents, he was a big drinker. He smoked cigarettes—Bull Durham mostly—but when he lacked money he would sometimes tear paper from a paper sack and roll his own. He was witty, had a crooked smile, along with a sparkle in his blue eyes—possibly from his enjoyment of drinking. He would hold the bottle up to the light after every drink.

He shared his parents' superstitious nature and sometimes discussed a belief in the supernatural. He referred to ghosts as "haints," invoking a term commonly used in the southern United States at the time.

As a younger man he was known as a big gambler, and some of his poker games got out of hand. Earl recalled a scar across the back of his dad's neck, as the result of being cut by his brother-in-law during a poker game. Jim W. wasn't known to hesitate in using his knife either, and he once shot a man who attempted to run away with the game's winnings. He never backed down then, and this trait did not change as he got older.

In 1945, when Earl was on furlough, he saw his dad come home after being hit with a beer bottle in a fight. His head had a cut which appeared to almost scalp him, but he simply asked his son to put iodine on the wound and then went on about his business. Jim W. did slow down over time, but Earl recalled his dad still getting into scuffles even at the age of 65.

As a parent he was viewed as the kind disciplinarian who never scolded his children—he left that to his wife, Janie. If he got frustrated with Earl, he would say, "I guess you know your business, son." Earl saw his dad as being very tough and respected him as the head of the household. "Dad was the man of the house," Earl said. "When we'd eat dinner he always got the meat first back then." Earl recalled doing what he was told

Jim W. (on left) and brother Otis (on right) gambling with friends, circa 1910

to do; when he was 12, his dad had a bad tooth, which Earl pulled with pliers.

When he was young, after a night of drinking, Jim W. would occasionally get angry and mouthy, but he was largely known as a sweet drunk, who became calmer through the years. While living in Glasgow, he came home one night drunk, but with a surprise hidden in his overall's pocket for his young children, a fox terrier puppy they would come to name Spot. As a grandfather, he would sometimes pull out a pocket full of change and give it to his young grandchildren (but always raking back the quarters with his thumb).

Jim W. could be funny as well, although a lot of the time it was related to his drinking. Janie would have to hide the banjo when he came home drunk because he would always want to play. Payday was especially bad when he came home; Janie would have to remove the crank handle from the Victrola record player because he would always love to do some soft-shoe tap dancing along with playing the humorous traditional American folk song "Ida Red," ("Ida Red, Ida Red, I'm a plum fool 'bout Ida Red").

Once, in later years, Jim W. came to visit Earl. Jim W. had been drinking a lot earlier that evening and during the middle of the night he woke up eager for a beer. When he went to open the refrigerator, he became mad because he thought someone had purposely removed the handle. He didn't know it was an old International refrigerator that was opened by a foot pedal.

Jim W. had little formal education, only third grade, and could barely write his name (he still knew the beer signs though he couldn't read). Janie eventually taught him how to write his name legibly.

He didn't drive, but he found rides or used public transportation to get around. At age 66, Jim W. eventually retired with a small pension from B.F Goodrich in Louisville, after fourteen years working as a plant painter.

After retirement, he painted houses with his teenage grandson David, who bought a motor scooter with the money he saved. The scooter came in handy because he used it later to give his grandfather rides to the local bowling alley so he could drink beer.

When he was near death, Jim W. confided in his granddaughter, Dolores, who worked in education, that his biggest regret was that he never learned to read or write. He was a humble and considerate person and looked at death the same way he lived his life. Jim W. summed things up for himself with these final words: "Well, I've had my fun, and it's time for me to go on and make room and a job for the young people."

Jim W. in yard at Falls of Rough, circa 1942

While Earl was growing up, it was the Prohibition era; the money Jim W. spent on his drinking always had to be checked, especially on the days he got paid. Still, Jim W. provided for his family the best he could during the toughest of times. With his painting and odd jobs, he somehow was also able to save enough (maybe along with some bartering) to get Ruth a piano. Carl learned to play as well, mostly by ear.

During those days, it was still very difficult for everyone in the home. The Great Depression had begun and unemployment in the country had risen to 25 percent, but in certain areas it was much higher. The city of Louisville saw unemployment peak at almost 35 percent during this time.

"Dad was a painter," Earl recalled, "but there was no work in the winter. We paid a full sum of 21 dollars a month for rent and we got three months behind. We had a very good landlord. Dad talked him into letting us paint the house and the roof for the three months' rent. That was back when Cokes were a nickel, but no one had a nickel. Life was tough. During the winter sometimes, Carl and I even dug under the fence at 29th and Griffith in Louisville to get into a coal yard and steal coal because we were so cold. There was no money. It was a pretty hard life.

"When I went to school, I wouldn't eat in the school cafeteria because I never had any money. It was hard to find food so Carl and I would go down to the hydroelectric plant and catch the stunned fish just passing through the dam." The hydroelectric plant consisted of a series of locks and a dam located at the Falls of the Ohio. "The fish would come out on the surface of the water and we'd shoot them with our BB guns. We were glad to have fish to eat, but the only thing we caught was carp. Carp, just mostly rooted in the mud for food, and weren't the best of fish to eat. We didn't know that's what we were eating, but Mom always made extra corn bread when we would eat those fish.

"When it came to clothes, I had a pair of shoes and two pairs of pants. When Mom washed one pair, I'd put on the other. Corduroy or moleskin pants were worn a lot because of the warmer material. We didn't wear blue jeans then. I wore those pants out from wearing them so much. I also wore rubber boots for a year once and didn't want people to know, so I pulled my pant legs down over them as far as they'd go."

Chapter Two

JANIE

Earl's mother, Lottie Jane, known as Janie (D.O.B. August 31, 1888) was born to Hannah Elizabeth England and James Calloway Denham on a farm in Tompkinsville, Kentucky, just as her parents before her.

The Denham family had a long, but complex military history. Janie's grandfather Allen C. Denham, was from Tennessee, a state that belonged to the Confederacy. At around age 45, he enlisted voluntarily in Kentucky to fight for the Union during the Civil War. He later became a Baptist minister. Her great-grandfather, Alexander P. Denham, was born in South Carolina to Northern Irish immigrants of Scottish descent. He fought in the war of 1812. After the war, he settled in Mississippi, where he owned a plantation.

Janie's sister Bernette, and her adopted daughter Alice, circa 1910

Alexander was named after his grandfather, who had immigrated to America, bringing his son James to South Carolina, but as an Irish southern loyalist, fought alongside the British during the Revolutionary War.

Janie's brother Oscar, top row (l.), circa 1887

Janie was the youngest of eight children: Bernette, William, Oscar, Ural, Isaac, Isabelle, and Francis. Janie experienced frequent tragedy that began early on. When she was two, her mother, just one month shy of her 35th birthday, died during childbirth. She gave birth to a son named Levi, but he died three weeks later. The other children left behind ranged in age from three to 13.

Pulmonary Tuberculosis (TB), a bacterial infection, began sweeping the nation, an epidemic that became known as the Great White Plague. It hit the Denhams hard. When she was nine years old, Janie's father died from TB at age 42. In 1913, the disease claimed her sister, who was 31 and married with two young children. Ten years later, her sister Isabelle, married with four children, was institutionalized in St. John's Tuberculosis Sanitarium in Springfield, Illinois, where she stayed for two years until her death at age 37. Five years later, Isabelle's husband, an alleged rumrunner, who used the rivers for transporting liquor, was slain during a gun duel. The children, having lost both parents, were forced to live for a time in an orphanage.

The youngest brother of the Denham family, Isaac, did not contract TB, but was institutionalized at the Louisville Central Kentucky Lunatic Asylum (later Central State Hospital) at age 15, possibly from dealing with

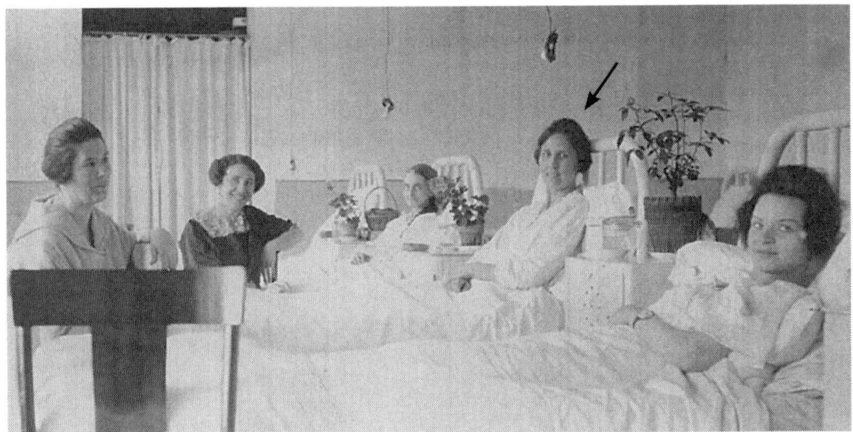

Isabelle, sick with TB, circa 1925

St. John's TB Sanitorium

Janie's sister Francis, circa 1910

the loss of his mother and father. Things worsened from there; Isaac died in 1918 at age 33 from a fall-related seizure. The coroner suspected foul play because of the observed trauma, but nothing was ever confirmed.

Isaac's older brothers experienced many of the difficulties of the time period. Oscar became a servant and laborer for a Tompkinsville family, and later he rented a small piece of property to begin farming. William and Ural, living in central Illinois and working on farms, were drafted, at ages 40 and 34, to fight in WWI. Both made it home safely and returned to Illinois.

When Janie's parents died, the family had been living on the farm where her father James had been born and raised. They had previously lived on several farms in Kentucky, but this property was inherited by James upon the death of his parents.

After her parents' death, Janie went to live and to be cared for by her oldest sister Bernette, who was then nineteen and married. The other children went to live with family members or set off on their own, working as servants.

Janie had to grow up quickly during those times. She learned to quilt by age nine, and at age 11 she was hired as a live-in cook for a young

Janie with a boyfriend, circa 1906

Tompkinsville couple and their two children. Bernette was a housekeeper and, by age 14, Janie began cleaning houses, and living with those people for whom she worked, including a local judge and a doctor in Tompkinsville.

While growing up, Janie did what most women weren't allowed to do during that time: she smoked, wore pants, and even used makeup. She also could be seen riding a horse astride instead of riding side saddle like women were accustomed to doing then. Sometimes, Janie would jump on a horse just to see if she could ride it. Family and friends viewed her as

Janie, circa 1903

someone who was very stubborn and tough in nature; she wasn't known to back down from anyone. It was her way or no way.

Despite her unconventional nature, she still had many male suitors. Janie completed eight years of schooling, but it was known she mostly learned to read and write using the Bible and newspaper. After her father's death, the money from his estate was left to Janie and her sisters, but the trustee of the estate squandered it. By the time she turned 18, after the money was divided among her and her sisters, only a few hundred dollars remained in her trust fund.

She was tired of the small town life and took the money and moved to Kokomo, Indiana; on her 19th birthday, in 1907, she married a local man named Charles Athan. He was almost ten years older and owned the restaurant where she worked. But at the age of 23, she decided to leave him and return to Tompkinsville. He came to Tompkinsville and threatened legal action to force her to stop the divorce and return with him. He fought for a while, but ultimately to no avail. Mr. Athan eventually moved on and remarried in 1914.

Back in Tompkinsville, Janie needed work. Though her education qualified her to teach school, she was turned down. She was seen as a divorcee, which was frowned upon at the time. Janie eventually took a job at a restaurant that catered the local jail.

With her rebellious nature, Janie was probably drawn to someone like herself. Delivering meals to the jail, she met Jim W., who was 19, was in jail for either drinking, gambling, or fighting—maybe all three. They soon struck up a friendship, which continued after his release. Though it was unknown whether Charles had granted her the divorce yet, they married months later in 1912.

As a married couple, Janie and Jim W. argued a lot—mostly with her complaining about him, but they were still known to love one another (though during one intense argument, Jim W. ran to the bedroom and locked the door, then escaped out the window). It might be argued that Janie is why Jim W. drank so much.

Jim W. sometimes showed his displeasure with her support of President Roosevelt; when they argued, he'd say to his strong-willed and stubborn wife, "Have it my way, Janie. Have it my way." When frustrated with her, Jim W. referred to her as a hard-headed Dutchman (she was thought to be of Dutch decent, though genealogical information reveals her family was primarily of Scottish and English origin that included lineage who sailed on the initial Mayflower cruise to America.)

As she aged, Janie never was seen drinking any soda, even the popular Coca-Cola. She thought drinking soda was a sin and drank only tea and Postum, a caffeine-free coffee substitute. As a wife, she had a dim view of alcohol; she always found the liquor bottles that Jim W. hid and quickly poured them out, even those underneath the house, buried deep in coal piled in the basement, or under the top plate of the garage. When Jim W. wearing his long black overcoat, would walk up to house, she would beat it with a poker, trying to break any whiskey bottles he may have hidden in his pockets.

During WWII, all three brothers, though off fighting, tried to help their parents back home. They would always send money back home after payday. Even though they had sent money home, later they found that their parents hadn't spent it all, but saved some of it for their sons' return.

Like Jim W., Janie was quite superstitious. She would always exit the same door she entered, because she believed that otherwise bad spirits would follow you and good spirits stayed. Janie would invite her grandson, Charles, to come over on New Year's Day, because it was said to be good luck for the year if the first person into your home is a male. (Janie would definitely forbid a female to come in first). As a couple, Janie and Jim W. were sometimes known to sleep at the foot end of the bed. It was said that having your feet facing the door brought on misfortune. With such beliefs, when the first man landed on the moon in July 1969, Janie was sure it could not be real. Although not taken as seriously today, many superstitious beliefs still remain in the family.

Janie battled complications from diabetes and was legally blind in her later years. After Jim W. died in 1964, she lived alone, despite her poor eyesight; she was known to keep a sharp hatchet under her pillow for protection. Various family members still tell stories of their experiences with Janie. In her later years, surprisingly, Janie did soften, mostly because she missed Jim W. Brenda, one of her granddaughters, fondly recalls sitting and relaxing with her, simply listening to the radio and eating Cheerios. Janie passed away in the fall of 1970.

As a mother, Janie lived through tough times. Once, while living in Glasgow with her young children in the early 1920s, Janie was cooking dinner when she first saw the black bear that she was convinced was sleeping under the house. Janie swiftly hid her children in her wooden chifforobe and grabbed the shotgun. The bear didn't try to come in the house, so she didn't have to shoot.

Growing up, Earl recalled his mother as tough and a strict disciplinarian, even though she was very petite—about 4'11" and 95 lbs. Earl credited his mother for teaching him toughness, but also courtesy and respect. She passed down many rules, such as giving a firm handshake, and dictating that men should always remove their hats at the eating table. That's something you would soon find out if you ever ate with Earl, as his grandchildren especially can attest.

Janie was frequently ill, and spent a lot of time in bed after her youngest children were born. In later life, Earl believed that his mother's sickness was related to the onset of early menopause (he called it the "change of life"), but as a child he had no idea why she was so sick.

Even though she was sick a lot, Janie's children still had to follow her rules. She didn't lie and expected the same from her children. For persuasion, she often used a tree switch to get her children to properly behave. Case in point: when Earl was nine, he and his friend Raymond would find long cigarette butts in the street and they smoked them. Janie quickly figured it out, for although the family had little money, she made sure her children kept clean the best they could, and young Earl was made to take two baths a week. Since there was no running water, Earl would carry water in from outside, heat it on the wood stove, and fill the galvanized steel bath tub to begin his bath. What he didn't realize once was that Janie had smelled smoke on him earlier.

"I was taking a bath and Mom busted in and asked me if I had been smoking, I said, no ma'am, then, yes ma'am—I didn't know what to say. She stood me up and began to whip me with a switch up and down the back of my back and legs. Every time she whipped one of us kids she'd say 'I am going to cut the blood out of you and rub salt in the gashes.' She didn't whip real hard, but it would still be child abuse these days. I deserved it and I never touched a cigarette from then on."

Chapter Three

SPECIAL SISTERS

The age difference between Jim W. and Janie's children was typically about 34 months. Ruth, the oldest, was a teenager at the time when her mother became sick, and during her high school years she became something of a surrogate mother and caregiver to her younger siblings, Carl, Earl, and Nina. Ruth was cooking and cleaning for the family by the age of eight. Earl recalled her many times sitting outside over a wash tub, scrubbing his clothes on a wooden scrub board. She was also known to patch up her father after a wild night of drinking and card playing that maybe had led to a fight. Sometimes she had to break up one of her parents' many arguments so none of the younger kids would have to do it.

Even at the end of his life, Earl still remembered what his sister had done for him. "She was a great influence in raising me," he said, "and was a mother to all of us. I thanked her many times for what she did for me."

Like the rest of her family, Ruth was tough from the start. She had been sick as a child and teenager, surviving both tuberculosis and scarlet fever, with doctors not expecting her to live past 20. Ruth spent time at a sanitarium and was then allowed by the doctors to heal at home; she slept apart from family with the window left open, even during the winter, for the fresh air that was supposed to help with her healing. As an adult, she was diagnosed with colon cancer, but she still lived another 27 years.

Aunt Isabelle (Bea), Ruth, and Bill, circa 1917

Ruth was intelligent and exhibited artistic and creative sides. She was a good seamstress and could make about anything. As a young girl she once won a city-wide art contest with a painting. The story goes that she could have taken the painting to a national audience if it had been done in oil, but the family was poor, so she could only afford water-based paint. Ruth dropped out of high school her senior year to begin working full time; that was common then.

Ruth as a flapper in high school, circa 1930

As an adult, Ruth married husband Charles (Wilbur) Allen, and maintained her caregiver ways, mostly staying home to raise

Ruth and Wilbur, circa 1948

their six children: Charles, Dolores, Marilyn, James, Richard, and Sharon. However, when WWII was in full swing, she worked at a Louisville airplane parts factory to help with the war effort.

As a young woman, Ruth joined the Order of Eastern Star, a fraternal organization for both men and women members based on teachings from the Bible. She was kind hearted and knew what it was like to grow up without much, so she would help others the best way she could. Ruth also had a sense of humor and was known for many sayings such as, "I understand all I know and I stand under all I know," and "Every stitch you sew on Sunday, you will have to remove with your nose on Judgment Day." These sayings were accompanied with strong body language.

After the death of Wilbur, Ruth worked as a nurse's aide at a well-known children's hospital in Louisville. Ruth fell in love with her work and was known to excel beyond what her job required or allowed, even learning to easily start an intravenous medication (IV) line in children's small veins. More than one doctor, knowing her skill, deferred that task to her. In later years, one of her biggest regrets was not finishing high school and attempting to further her education, because she knew she could have become a great nurse.

Growing up, Earl was also very close to his sister Nina, who always helped him with something he never enjoyed, his homework. He credited her for helping him get through to the sixth grade and he recalled her never tattling to their parents when he got disciplined at school for fighting, which was a lot. At Short Creek High School, she met a boy from Falls of Rough named Tommy Allen, a cousin of her brother-in-law, Wilbur, and they began dating. Dating was difficult for Nina because Tommy would have to come to her house. They would sometimes sit and look at a Sears & Roebuck catalogue, but if Janie, sitting close by in

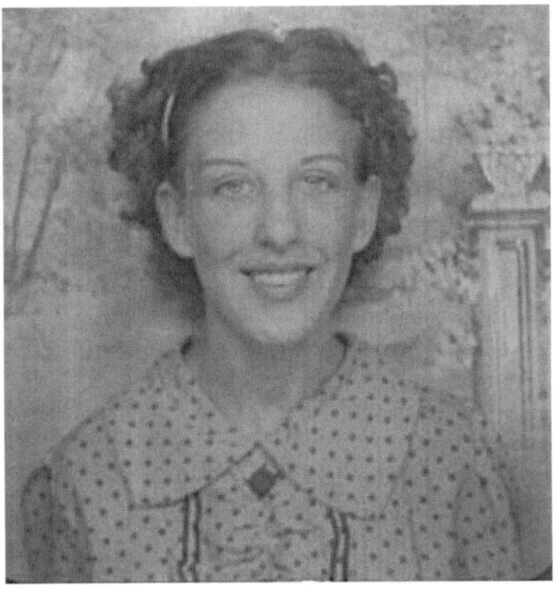

Nina as a teenage girl, circa 1936

the other room, didn't hear the pages turning, she'd yell at her daughter. "Nina, what are you doing?"

Nina planned to marry Tommy, but she was only 16, and her mom strongly opposed the marriage because of her age and because she was the baby of the family. Janie even wrote to Earl, who was in Hawaii with the Navy, about this.

Nina and Tommy, circa 1942

"Mom wrote me that Nina planned to get married and wanted me to come home and stop it," Earl said, "I know it made her mad a little, but I told her I was four thousand miles from home. There was nothing I could do."

Nina and Tommy eventually eloped in Caneyville, and the marriage ceremony was performed by Ruth's father-in-law and Methodist minister, Lafe Allen. Janie found out and was on her way to stop it, but she was too late. After the wedding, she urged Jim W. to attempt to get the marriage quickly annulled, but to no avail. Janie was even angry at Carl because he approved of the marriage and didn't try to intervene.

Tommy and Nina would have three children, David, Brenda, and Rhonda. Like most people then, Nina and Tommy didn't have much money, and Tommy was soon drafted into the Army to fight in the South Pacific during World War II. Nina was always a homemaker and a perfectionist in how her home ran and appeared. She was a loving and caring parent, but expected her children to behave respectfully both in the home and outside of it. She also shared her parents' superstitious nature—definitely no singing in bed or rocking an empty rocking chair in Nina's house.

Nina adopted her mother's strict view of parenting. Nina saw loved ones join the military with her three older brothers and she understood what being a part of the United States military meant. When her oldest child, David, joined the Army before the Vietnam War, she cried when the recruiter pulled up to take him away. David remembers returning after six years of service and buying a motorcycle. His mother, caring, but still strict, showed concern and anger when she voiced her displeasure: "I thought the Army straightened you out, but now you have bought a motorcycle."

Though strict like her mother, Nina had her father's sense of humor. Nina's youngest daughter, Rhonda, recalls a fond memory as a young girl, of her mom showing her humorous side. Once, while arguing with her mom and becoming angry, Rhonda told her, "I hope you wake up with rocks in your pillow!" The next morning, Rhonda awoke to her mother in her bedroom, hiding her amusement along with the dirt and dust on her hands, pointing to the rocks in Rhonda's pillow (which seem to have gone missing from an artificial plant in the house). Rhonda, seeing that her wish hadn't come true, and because she now had rocks in her own pillow, regretted her words.

Nina also liked to take her children to Fontaine Ferry Park. Most of the rides scared Nina, but she loved the Ferris wheel. She was known to have a little fun when riding it with her children, by gently (and safely) rocking it back and forth, just playfully scaring her children a little bit.

Because she married young, Nina was just short of graduating high school. That made it more important to her that her children graduated. When she found she had cancer and it progressed, she made Rhonda, who was 14 at the time, promise she would graduate high school.

Nevertheless, Nina was intelligent and skilled, like her parents and siblings before her, and she grew smart from the hard life-lessons she learned growing up poor. A talented seamstress, she made clothes for her family, and she was a natural painter. Nina, a Bluegrass music fan, could also pick a little mandolin to play along with her favorite songs on the radio.

Ruth and Nina were similar in many ways and also very close. When Nina was diagnosed with colon cancer, her sister Ruth decided to go ahead and get checked out as well. Nina had problems for a long time prior to this, but had been misdiagnosed. It turned out Ruth and Nina battled colon cancer simultaneously, though Nina's was far more progressed. A little less than two years and five surgeries after being diagnosed, she died at the young age of 46 and only two months after the death of her mother, Janie. Both losses, in such short order, hit the family hard.

To his dying day, Nina's older brother Earl had a special place in his heart for his younger sister. "Looking back on my sisters, Ruth was more of a mother to me, but Nina was a sister all the way and a fine lady and person," he said. "Whatever good things a person can say about her, they will never be exaggerating."

Earl's family pegged him with many nicknames throughout his life. Nina and Ruth's children and a few others called him Uncle Pete or Pete, a name they still used until the day he died. No one recalls the origin of the name, but Earl was fine with it. "I don't know why they have always called me that; it was something they just did," he said. "I never minded; I always had a great relationship with all those kids."

Chapter Four

MISCHIEVOUS OR JUST ADVENTUROUS

The Smith family was not Catholic, but once they moved to Louisville near the Churchill Downs race track, and maybe for disciplinary reasons, Earl attended a Catholic grade school for a short time. He then attended J.B. Atkinson Elementary in the West End, then Western Junior High School (Western Middle School today).

Earl, as a young kid, was in trouble a lot, mostly for fighting. "I wasn't a bully. I just never liked me or anybody else to be made fun of, and I would stand up to whoever that did it," Earl said.

In grade school at Atkinson Elementary, Earl's principal was Mrs. Grunder, who wore all black and could be mean. She was known to the students as "Grunder the Thunder," because of her strict discipline. Mrs. Grunder sometimes rapped Earl's knuckles with a ruler, and would make him wear a dunce cap, sitting in the hallway's Goon's chair when he would fight. She had two chairs for punishment, but Earl usually sat alone. Once sitting, all of his schoolmates, as they walked by, pointed at him and chuckled. Sometimes this punishment wasn't enough and he would be sent to the cloak room to sit alone, with his teacher always trying to make an example out of him.

The threat of punishment didn't seem to affect Earl because he continued to be mischievous in school. Once, when a student who sat in front of Earl was reciting standing beside his desk, Earl, from behind him reached forward and jerked his knickers down. That drew laughter from everyone except the teacher and the embarrassed student.

Because Earl and Carl were brothers, and also close in age, they were natural allies who were always looking for fun. As kids, though Earl was younger but bigger than Carl, some people on occasion thought they were twins. Earl and Carl tried to have fun like most, but entertainment was sometimes limited because of the hard times living in Louisville.

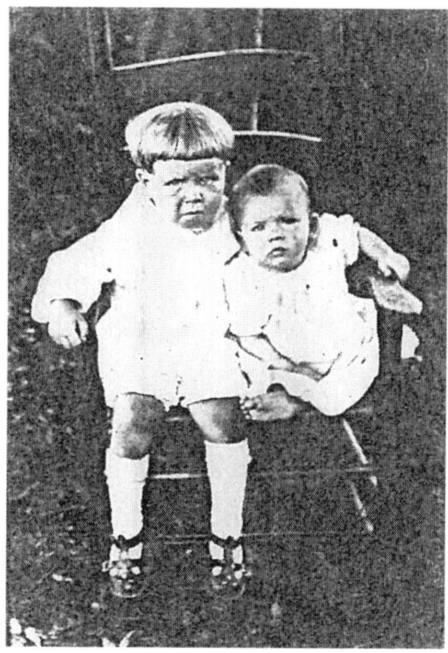

Carl (l.) and Earl (r.) as a toddler and baby, 1921

"We didn't have entertainment like we do today; we never had or listened to a radio growing up. We could go and see movies at the local theaters for 10 cents; we'd go over to 4th St. and Shawnee. We could go up to Fontaine Ferry Park at the foot of Market Street when we had the money. They had amusement rides and a swimming pool. We rode the Idlewild, (which) later became the Belle of Louisville on the Ohio. We rode it over to Rose Island in Indiana once. It was a popular local amusement park then… about 14 miles up. (It) took around two hours to get there, but it was worth the wait.

"For fun, we made our own fun mostly. In grade school we would do mischievous things for fun. Carl and I just rode bikes, so sometimes we'd mess with the street cars. We'd go down to Alford Street in Louisville. We found a way by just watching the conductor, to be able to move this pulley with a rope. This pulley was attached to a wire, the power source. We learned how to make those street cars stop with the rope on the back of the car; I was able to tug on it a little to take the pulley off the wire all by myself. It would immediately stop when I would do it, the conductor would jump off so fast and come to the back of the car so mad. Carl and I would run and sometimes he'd even run after us. He wasn't very happy," Earl said as he laughed.

The two brothers, becoming even braver, weren't done harassing the street cars. At the end of the day when school would let out, Earl and Carl, on their way home, would sometimes lay across the tracks, playing a game of chicken with the conductor. The frustrated conductor had no choice, but to always have to stop. Earl, looking back and laughing at the memory, admitted doing that wasn't very smart, but he remembered being always ready to quickly spring up.

Streetcar in Louisville, circa 1930

Many of Earl and Carl's adventures came from Carl's knack for money making. Their oldest brother William (Bill) had a job selling newspapers for the *Herald-Post* in Louisville and Carl was eager to become a newspaper boy like his brother. The district manager decided to hire him. In July of 1931, with Bill's blessing, the manager turned over Bill's carrying route 3606 to Carl and transferred Bill to 3605. Carl sold copies of the *Herald-Post,* on the corner at 26th and Portland. When that paper went out of business, he started selling *The Courier-Journal* on Sunday and *The Louisville Times* through the week. Bill was also a carrier for the Courier and the Times, (The Bingham family owned both papers, the C-J in the morning, Times in the afternoon.)

The paper cost five cents; the boys would take two cents home for each delivery made. Though they just earned pennies from their deliveries, the money from the two paper routes became important—it helped keep the family going during that winter.

Also, during that summer, Carl built a two-wheel push cart and he began getting up at 4:00 a.m. every day, to push it three miles to Louisville's Haymarket (farmer's market), where he bought five bushels of assorted vegetables to peddle on the street for a small profit. Earl sometimes went along to help out. The next summer, Carl's vegetable business became bigger; he bought a pony and a wagon to haul and sell 12 bushels.

Carl, now the "money man," even at his young age, saved up enough money from selling papers and vegetables to buy a Model T Ford, and then moved up with a two-door dual bench seat Chevrolet Roadster. It was Bill who drove them around, but once when Earl was 12 years old, Carl made the mistake of letting him get behind the wheel.

"Bill was gone one day and Carl says, 'Let's go get some gas,' Earl recalled. "He said, 'Earl, you drive.' There was no such thing as a driver's license then or a license plate. There was no such thing as insurance on your vehicle. So, we drove to 26th and St. Xavier. We pulled in, and the gas pumps were on a concrete island. Whoever was there before I was didn't hang the hose up properly. They let the hose hang out on the pavement off the island. When I went in I didn't hit the island, but I ran over the hose; I busted it pretty good."

Carl loaned Earl the money to pay for a new hose, because the commonly used natural rubber, which was so expensive at the time, it cost over three dollars to replace; that was big money in those days. In return, Earl helped Carl deliver papers. Then, after he paid off Carl, Earl got his own paper route.

That wasn't the first (or last) adventure the two of them had. Before long they found themselves living, along with their family, on a small farm in west central Kentucky, then solo in a neighboring town thanks to another of Carl's ventures.

CHAPTER FIVE

A NEW HOME IN FALLS OF ROUGH

Smith Purchases Farm With Money Saved From Route

CARL SMITH.

Buys Six-Acre Farm In Grayson County; Plans Getting More Land.

Few boys become land owners before they attain their majority, but one ambitious carrier has become not only a property owner, but a farmer as well.

Carl Smith, carrier of Route [illegible], bought a six-acre tract of land near Falls of Rough, Grayson County, Kentucky, and completed arrangements for planting crops on the property. The farm, on which is located a three-room house and a barn, is being taken care of by a relative who owns an adjoining property.

About three years ago, William Smith, Carl's older brother, was carrying Route [illegible] for The Times and Sunday Courier-Journal. Carl was eager to become a newspaper boy and on July 11, [illegible], John [illegible], district manager, turned over the route to Carl, transferring William to Route [illegible].

Carl immediately began to save the earnings from his route and soon had a bank account of more than $100. In February, Carl, with his family, took a trip to Grayson County, where he had an opportunity to see the property he now owns. He was eager to invest his savings and soon was in possession of the deed.

The youthful farmer said he made a good deal and provided a home for his father and mother. He plans to buy more land from time to time with earnings from his route.

Carl was absent from school for the first time in six years in February, as the time he was away from the city. He is in the eighth grade at Western Junior High School.

Earnings from Carl's route also were used to purchase his own clothes. Carl maintained a splendid record during his entire period of service as a carrier for The Courier-Journal and The Louisville Times.

Carl is a son of Mr. and Mrs. J. W. Smith, [illegible] St. Xavier Street.

Schnurr Commended On Splendid Record

May 1932 article about Carl purchasing land. Taken from The Hustler-Falls *Cities Edition (owned by the* Courier-Journal *and* Louisville Times)

One day the Smith brothers' long lost cousin showed up at their house. J.C. Paige, Janie's nephew, was the son of her sister Francis who died from tuberculosis at age 31. He was then 23, and had tracked down the Smith family to let them know how he was doing. J.C., who later died of tuberculosis at age 26, had married a girl from Caneyville in Grayson County, and somehow convinced Carl, who was 13, to pay 100 dollars for a six acre farm in nearby Falls of Rough, nearly 95 miles southwest from Louisville.

The Great Depression began on Oct. 29, 1929, as the result of the stock market crash. Black Tuesday, as it was known, resulted in 10,000 banks eventually failing by 1932.

"Most of the banks went under because of the Depression," Earl recalled, "but Carl's bank at 26th and Bank Street in Louisville didn't. He still had that 100 dollars. We started going down

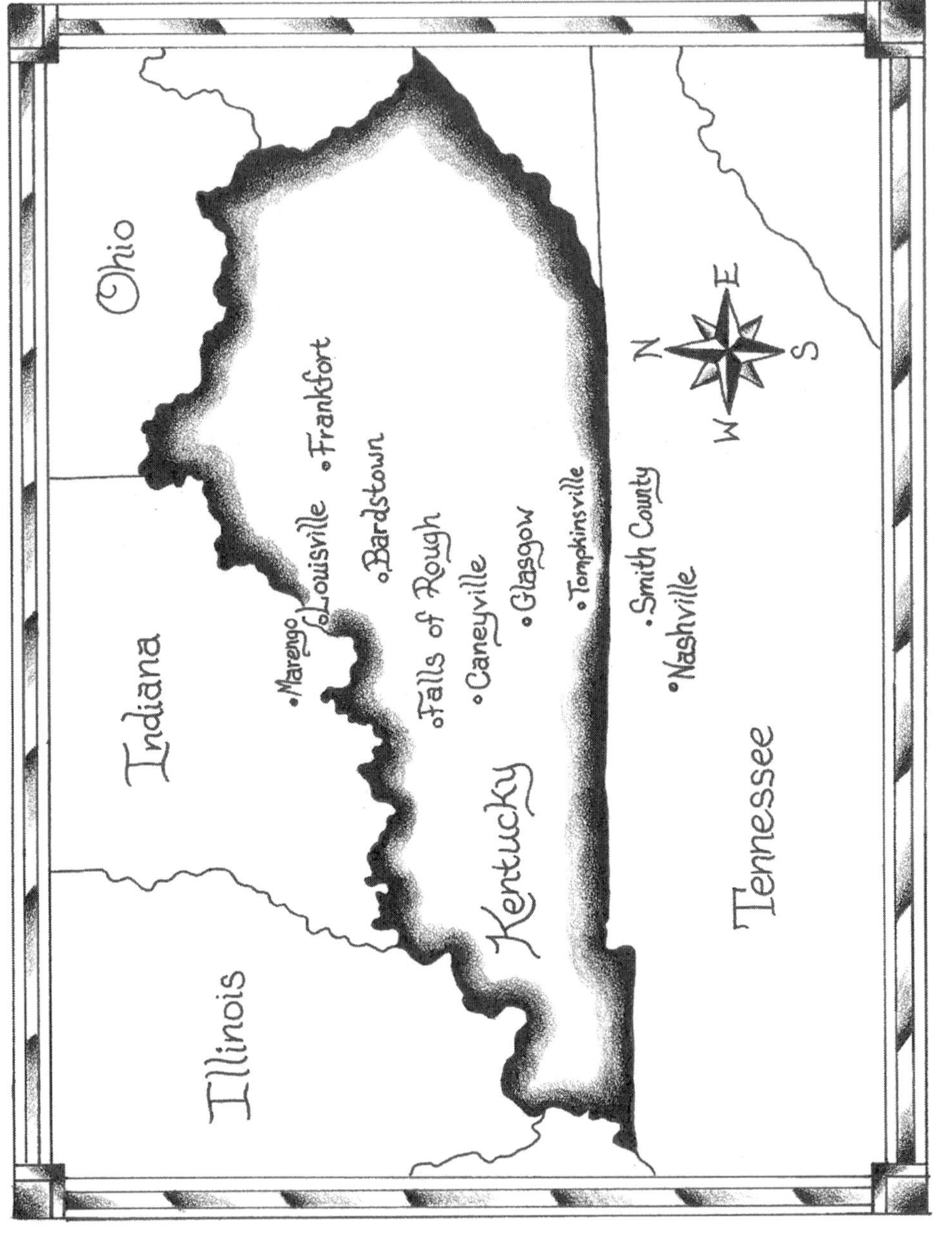
Ohio
Indiana
Illinois
Kentucky
Tennessee
Frankfort
Bardstown
Louisville
Marengo
Falls of Rough
Caneyville
Glasgow
Tompkinsville
Smith County
Nashville
N
E
S
W

there (to Falls of Rough) on Sunday morning after delivering papers. It seemed we'd be gone from home most of the day; we'd go down there and stay three or four hours, enough to have a little fun, then we'd make the trip back."

This went on until the family was forced to move out there. "We couldn't afford the six to nine dollars a month rent for our little shotgun house in Louisville and had to move down there," Earl said. "I think some of the reason was because of Mom's health, too. Dad thought fresh country air would help her."

Falls of Rough, sometimes simply called, "The Falls," was a slow-paced rural town with an estimated population of 250 to 300 people. The town sat next to Rough River and took its name from the rapids. One of the town's signature landmarks was a single-lane bowstring arched steel bridge, just less than 147 feet, stretching across the Rough River which separated Grayson and Breckinridge counties. The 1877 bridge is the oldest of its architectural type currently in Kentucky; it overlooked a dam and once functioning gristmill below.

Falls of Rough Bridge, circa 1950

Earl recalled as a youngster walking the nearly two mile walk to the river. Sometimes he stopped on the bridge and watched curiously if someone was being baptized down below.

Carl and Earl slept in the attic of the small three-room house; the new farm also had a henhouse and a barn. Addresses weren't in use back then, and the house was simply called the "white house," from the white-wash paint that covered it, sometimes sparingly. It had only a wooden door latch, but they didn't worry about break-ins. There was a ladder up to the attic, where they could see the tin roof overhead, and a small hole was cut in the floor in an attempt to capture rising heat from the stove. There was no running water, no electricity, and not even a mattress. They got water from a nearby spring, and to see at night, they used coal oil lanterns. They all slept on corn shucks, including Bill, who later joked that young Earl wet the bed, which kept him warm at night. The corn shucks ruffled against each other and the noise made it difficult for them to sleep. The house was insulated by burlap sacks that hung on the studs, with wallpaper placed over the sacks.

The winter of 1932-1933 was so cold, with temperatures dropping below zero, that the boys moved their bed to the kitchen to sleep next to the wood stove. The boys admitted that sometimes the stove would be out by morning, they were too tired to keep feeding it wood during the night. Eventually, Carl bought some rough beech lumber and hired a neighbor with a team of mules and a wagon to haul it up to the farm. The teenager then hired another man, who worked for 50 cents a day, to put a better insulated rolled roof on the house, tear away the kitchen, and add two rooms. The man, with just the use of a hand saw, built the rooms, along with added detail.

During the Great Depression, the Smith family, like most families, was just trying to survive. Earl recalled the struggle of life in Falls of Rough that was similar to most American towns and cities during that time. "There was no money then," Earl explained. "Those who still had it, kept it out of circulation. The biggest problem was food. There were bread lines, and food lines, with so many waiting. We had to eat a lot of wild rabbits to survive. I remember many nights going to bed with a glass

Bread line, circa 1935

of buttermilk and cornbread, but I wasn't hungry just eating that. I guess I was used to it."

With his family living in Falls of Rough, Jim W. continued trying to pick up whatever work he could. He stayed back in Louisville, mostly for work opportunities, and tried to come down on weekends. Laborers were often paid an hourly rate of just nine cents. As a professional painter, during the summer months, he could sometimes find work out of Louisville, and he once painted the single-lane bridge in Falls of Rough for two dollars a day. The initial offer was one dollar, but he held out based on his professional

Falls of Rough bridge, circa 1935

skills. Jim W., with a paint brush in one hand and sometimes a whiskey flask in the other, painted the bridge with skill, strapped and hanging off the side. There were no complaints about his work after he finished.

Falls of Rough was a hardworking community; people could be seen out in the fields working, and the daytime air was usually filled with noise from the local sawmill, as saw blades ripped into tree logs. For entertainment, families and neighbors visited each other; during the warmer months, children could be seen watching local baseball games. Neighbors weren't in close proximity; visiting often required long walks and wading shallow streams. The fields, woods, and brush thickets had multiple paths worn from constant travel, and at night you could see the coal oil lanterns glowing as residents moved between houses.

Men working in the fields wore overalls, shirts buttoned up to the neckline and straw hats to protect them from hot summer sun. On Sundays or for social outings, men wore a suit and tie along with a brimmed dark hat. Most men who owned a suit only had one.

In town, women wore home-sewn simple dresses (usually covered with an apron if at home) made out of durable wool or cotton. Some were lucky if they had an additional dress for church, weddings, or family gatherings. Many times dresses were made out of flour or feed sacks, especially after sacks came out in colored variations.

Children wore hand-me-down overalls, knickers, or corduroy pants, along with a flat cap, and a straw or black brimmed hat in summer. Because nobody had much money for new clothes, patches sometimes eventually covered patches.

Falls of Rough also had strong spiritual beliefs; Earl remembered the old-timers sitting on the front porch playing music and discussing the Bible. Many times the children played fiddle. One of Earl's favorite songs was "Shall We Gather at the River," which he once heard while standing outside a local church funeral of an older man in town who he knew. He was around age 13 at the time, but because he was embarrassed because of a large rip in the seat of his pants covered by a worn-out patch, he thought it wasn't respectful for him to go inside.

Earl had many friends to hang out with and he would often visit the Eskridge family, who had five daughters and a son. As they grew older, the girls became very popular with the boys in town. Earl recalled their father as a big gambler, who was gone a lot. It was still the Prohibition era, and Earl would talk to the children's bootlegging uncle, a big man, who he recalled wore rubber boots year around to conceal the booze he peddled.

Earl also frequently visited his neighbor, a man about his dad's age,who they called Uncle Maine. Earl had another reason to visit Maine, because his son, Sol, was Earl's best friend. Earl enjoyed visiting them and singing popular Bible-based songs along the way, catching lightning bugs in a jar, and even the times when he had to crawl through thick brush to get there. Uncle Maine's real name was Marion Allen, but in their

Earl (r.) and Sol (l.) as kids, circa 1932

slow speaking country drawl, the locals simplified the pronunciation over time.

Once Earl became a teenager, he enjoyed attending pie suppers at the local school. Pie suppers were social gatherings where pies were auctioned to raise money. Girls donated homemade pies, sometimes decorated with ribbons and bows, and the highest bidder won the prize of sharing the pie with its maker, whose identity was usually concealed. Earl remembered the suspense to the bidding, because it had a courtship element, as boys vied to win a pie and learn the identity of the girl who baked it.

The Illinois Central Railroad, a freight train, would stop in Caneyville, which was about 12 miles south of Falls of Rough, to fill up with water to power the steam engine. Earl and Carl would walk to the station and catch the train for the nearly 90-mile ride to Louisville that ended at 5th and Hill Streets. Though they usually went together, they sometimes went alone as well. The brothers sometimes rode up on Friday after school and returned when the train stopped, 11:30 Sunday night. With the long journey in complete darkness, it sometimes took five hours to return home.

Jim W. would catch the train periodically, riding there with his young sons. Sometimes the train wasn't on time or didn't stop for water (the load it carried determined how much water was needed). One time Earl needed to catch a train to Louisville and get five dollars from Jim W. But the train didn't stop that time, and not knowing anyone in Caneyville, he simply turned around and walked 12 miles back home.

Even if the train didn't stop, if it slowed down enough, Carl and Earl could jump on and jump off while it was in motion. But sometimes, part of the journey of getting there wasn't too pleasant for the young brothers.

Shane's store, circa 1935

The boys usually took a back way through woods and fields, sometimes following a worn path locals called the "run." They eventually would travel down a road full of attractions. It was a dirt road, with Shane's general store in close proximity. Shane's had daily necessities, but also open wooden barrels of crackers out front for sale, which was common for general stores of the time. There was also a small one-room store and gas station owned by George Fentress that mostly sold canned goods, deli sandwiches, and drinks. Earl and Carl had to walk through a small creek, Pleasant Run, which passed over the road; the spot was used as the local car wash and even a hangout. Always hungry, they had a chance to grab a bite to eat courtesy of an apple orchard. Earl mostly enjoyed the long walk, until they approached two cemeteries.

"We'd always have to walk along the edge of two cemeteries," Earl said, laughing at the memory. "When I would walk past, my hair would stick up like a dog and my feet would get light. I knew in my mind nothing was in there but dead people, and nothing could hurt us. I was still scared though; as a young kid I thought that place was full of ghosts."

ORIGINAL TAX BILL FOR
BUDGET YEAR 1934-1935

GRAYSON COUNTY No 2362

From January 1, 1935 to June 30, 1935,
Inclusive

Due by Smith Jane Dist. No. 3

No. ______ Street ______ Ky.

COUNTY TAX

	As Equalized		Tax
Exemptions $			
Total real estate	$ 100	@ 25c	$ 25
Bank shares	$	@ 10c	$
Tangible personalty less exemptions	$	@ 25c	$
County poll		75c	$
TOTAL COUNTY TAX TO GENERAL FUND			$ 25
Road and bridge bond fund	$ 100	@ 10c	$ 10
6% penalty after February 28, 1935			$
6% interest after February 28, 1935			$
Advertising property distrained			$
Sheriff's ___ % for distraining			$
TOTAL OF ALL TAXES ~~WITH PENALTIES~~			$ 35

Certified as correct Mary [illegible] Clerk

Paid this 20 day of Mar 1936

[illegible] Sheriff by Preston [illegible] Deputy Sheriff

Tax receipt from farm

Chapter Six

THE GREEN FAMILY

One local family in Falls of Rough, while affected by the Depression, was still considered quite wealthy. The well-known Green family, which consisted of siblings Willis, Preston, Robert, and Jennie, owned many businesses in town, including the Green Brothers General Store that included two gravity flow gas pumps, a sawmill, blacksmith shop, and a gristmill, all sitting on or near Rough River. The family's land, Green Farms, initially purchased in 1821, totaled 6,000 acres of farmland, timber, and livestock.

Falls of Rough dam and the Green's mill, circa 1940

Sketch of Green family general store

The Green family mansion, 2011

The siblings, who were in their middle to late fifties and sixties at the time, lived in a two story house with 22 rooms that sat near the mill and general store. Built in 1828, it was considered a mansion; Earl admired the structure and was amazed by its size. None of the siblings married and they had no close relatives, so the money stayed directly among them. Earl estimated their net worth in the millions.

Willis Green, the oldest brother, suffered a bow-and-arrow accident as a child and had an artificial eye. Earl recalled that Willis played the wealthy Dapper Dan role and oversaw the operation of the family farm until his death in the middle 1940s. He didn't pay much attention to the local children, but Robert and Preston were down-to-earth and sociable with the children in town. Robert was the farm boss, Preston had lost a hand in a corn feeder, and he wore an artificial hand protected in a glove.

Earl recalled having a lot of fun with the two brothers. He rode around in Robert's car, and he would let Preston shoot his knuckles with

GREEN BROTHERS

Falls of Rough, Ky.

Clerk.......... Date 5-30 ....193 2

Name J. W. Smith

Address .... Am't Rec'd ....

3	Rolls Roofing	3	60
	Flour		65
	Matches		5
	Coffee		10
	Beans		10
		4	50

TO CORRECT ERRORS, BRING THIS BILL

Press of The National Cash Register Co., Dayton, Ohio

Receipt from the Green's general store
(note the three rolls of roofing for the farm house), 1932

a stone marble as part of a game they played. This went on down at the general store, where Preston would buy Earl a coke as a reward for being a good sport.

Carl and Preston loved pitching horseshoes, and they often did it together. Carl eventually became horseshoe champion in Falls of Rough from all their practice. He always respected the Green family—and for reasons more than their wealth. Typical of Carl's character, once, years later, Carl, who loved field corn, passed by the Green's corn field and picked an ear of corn and ate it. Though they would never know he took it, he made sure to leave a dime in the stalk.

Earl recalled a time that his father and brother-in-law Wilbur were out hunting and they ran into what they thought was a wild animal; they could only see its eyes coming towards them, and they were scared to death. They shot and killed the animal, which turned out to be one of the Greens' hogs.

"Dad and Wilbur got me to help drag it in at dark," Earl said. "They said they thought it was a wild animal ready to attack, but I knew they knew what it was. We were always hungry back then, and they knew the Greens wouldn't miss just one hog. They were still nervous when we went out to drag it home, though."

Though Earl got along well with the two Green brothers, he had a bad experience once with the sister, Jennie, who some might call eccentric. She was known to use her wealth for many extended trips to New York City and Europe. Jennie was always seen wearing green, from the clothes and hat she wore to the color of her chauffeur's clothing, and even the car driving her.

"I must have been 11 or 12 and was walking with my dog that was a shepherd looking dog; he always went everywhere I went," Earl said. "We were on the road walking along the fence in front of Green house; my dog began fighting with Jennie Green's three dogs. I was hissing for my dog to win, and all of the sudden Jennie Green climbed on that board fence and tried to slap at me. I didn't like her too much after that."

Many of the family's employees lived directly across Rough River in Breckinridge County, on what they called Booger Hill. Earl recalled a black friend who was a teenager about his age who lived with the Green family. The teen's older brother, Arthur, was a longtime employee. Earl's friend, named "Smoke," had the freedom to ride any pony or mule he wanted. Earl found that impressive, because he and the other children weren't even allowed on any of the grass and or to go beyond the white board fence.

Earl lost communication with the Green brothers after he joined the Navy, but Carl wrote letters to Robert for a short period. Even as he grew

The white board fence outside Green property, circa 1939

older, Earl always dreamed of walking on the Green Mansion property and seeing the inside. The three brothers each died in consecutive years and after the last sibling, Jennie, died in 1965, the mansion was willed to a distant cousin. Later, under new ownership, it became a bed and breakfast, and Earl, in his late 80s, had a dream come true when he toured the estate and stayed the night.

He said, "I have seen a lot, but I have waited 75 years to finally go in and see the mansion, and it was worth the wait. I couldn't even cross the white board fence as a kid."

Chapter Seven

MORE THAN JUST BROTHERS

As the oldest brother, Bill was almost five years older than Earl and was looked up to by his two younger brothers. Many times, they would just follow his lead. One Easter Sunday, while living in Glasgow, the Smith family's neighbor, Mr. Nelson, had an Easter egg hunt for all of his son's friends. Bill, who was around nine years old, watched him hide all the eggs, especially the prized speckled egg, worth 25 cents to the finder. Bill saw it being hid along the fence row and because his hand was too big, he persuaded Carl to slide his hand through and grab it. Carl did so, and all three brothers went behind the coal shed to each share a bite. The evidence, broken shell pieces, was then covered with dirt and since the egg was never found, the Nelson family dog received the blame.

Early on in life, Bill experienced some unpleasant times, beyond just being poor. When Bill was in grade school at Atkinson Elementary in Louisville, he stuttered, and his first grade teacher as punishment, sometimes would make him sit underneath her desk.

As a teenager, Bill was strong-willed, and sometimes knocked heads with his Dad, mostly when Jim W. was drinking. Bill was a high school football star, but several knee injuries prevented him from playing in college.

Also, Bill was no stranger to trouble. One time, while he was in high school and just before he entered the Navy, someone took a shot at him;

it missed, but the bullet went through his sport coat. He hid that from his mother. Earl remembered his older brother as a husky 17-year-old driving Carl's Model T to the movies, while wearing knickers like children wore in an effort to get the children's discount. From the start, that Model T seemed to create a lot of fun for the Smith brothers.

"We had many adventures with Bill and that ol' Model T," Earl said, laughing as he remembered how they handled various challenges, like getting stuck in the mud at the Falls when they would go down there on Sundays, back when Carl first bought the property. "Carl would drive, and Bill and I would always push to get through the mud," he said.

"To change tires, Bill would never jack it up, but just lift it up and sit it on the jack." When they were low on gas, which was all the time. Bill got creative. "The tank sat under the seat. To get up a hill, Bill would sometimes have to blow and push the gas into the carburetor, then block the hole made with the end of match-stick. If that didn't work, we'd just have to back up to push the gas forward. If Dad ever rode with us, he always had one foot on the running board, ready to jump out. We scared him; I think Dad thought his sons were a little crazy."

Bill was also very charismatic and witty, and his personality hardly changed in later life. He often wrapped a few dollars around a corncob to jokingly make people think he had a roll of bills. He became a little more serious with the trick when trying to impress a girl. Still, that role seemed to fit him, because in his later years he would dress as a clown for the Shriners to help raise money for children's and burn hospitals, along with an orphanage in Mexico.

By the time the family had moved to Carl's first farm down at Falls of Rough, Bill was 18 and had graduated from Manual High School. He'd decided to take Carl's Roadster out west. "Bill was wild and just wanted to go in that direction to see what he could see and get into," Earl said. "Bill and a friend headed out, but the car caught on fire in Nebraska and they hoboed back home, along with having to work a little along the way to get back. We'd already moved down to the Falls while he was gone, so he came back to the farm and stayed for what seemed like just a little while.

He had already enlisted in the Navy prior, but he was still waiting to be called up. They finally called him in '33."

When Bill left, Earl was in the ninth grade and attended school in a two-room school house, while Carl went to a better school in Short Creek, between Falls of Rough and Caneyville.

Earl recalled that, until the weather got too bad, Carl rode back and forth to school on a pony named King, which he'd traded for at Fontaine Ferry Park in Louisville. He boarded it for a dollar a week. Earl and Carl then moved to Caneyville, to take advantage again of a better school by "baching" it, living alone for a whole year. The two boys rented a small four-room house in Caneyville for three dollars a month. The house sat on about three acres that allowed them to keep a garden. Bill, now in the Navy, tried to help his young brothers survive by sending money each month.

Luckily for Carl and Earl, Ruth was living in Caneyville too. She had married Wilbur, and she had her oldest son Charles by then. She and Wilbur had met when Carl purchased his six acre farm and happened to get hung up in the mud while there. Wilbur helped him out and Ruth happened to be in the car. Wilbur's parents still lived there and it was also known as one of the cheaper places in the area to live.

Although her family was struggling like everyone else, Ruth was known as someone who knew how to manage the money they did have. She was a good cook and always seemed to have enough cornbread and beans around to share with her two hungry brothers. Ruth was always glad to see her brothers when they stopped by. Carl and Earl used to drop in on her regularly, because they had no money for school lunch.

Earl recalled having no transportation while living in Caneyville, but still courting a girl about seven miles away down a long dirt road leading deep into the woods. "My brother-in-law, Wilbur, gave me the keys on Sundays to go see her and to return that night; he trusted me," he said. "I got the enjoyment of driving a Willys-Knight automobile to go and see her; it was an Al Capone-looking car. I was only 13 or 14. I think I impressed her."

When Earl was 15, he was driving again and had an unforgettable experience. He was driving a 1928 Chevrolet sedan that Carl owned. Earl had to park the car a quarter mile away from his destination because of the heavy mud road up to the house. He drove up a hill next to some mailboxes and parked, but when he opened the door the brakes didn't lock. They gave out and the car began to roll back down. Earl tried to stop it, but the door caught on the mailboxes and broke off on its hinges. He was left holding the door in one hand when the car finally came to a stop.

Earl and Carl's house in Caneyville was about one mile and a half from the railroad station where the freight train stopped for water, a much shorter distance than the house in Falls of Rough. Still, the winter was very hard on Earl and Carl.

"In the winter time," Earl confessed, "when the freight train came through, that's the only stealing we ever did, was over coal." They would get on the coal car and throw off some coal and put what they could carry in a burlap sack, which they put in the back of Carl's 1928 Chevy. "We'd get enough coal to last us for a week and we spent two winters doing that. The winter of 1934 got below zero many times. Even without the wind, it felt like 35 degrees below. I don't know how we didn't freeze to death. It was stealing when we would take the coal, but we weren't the only ones doing it. We had to."

After moving to Caneyville, Earl and Carl continued hopping the freight train to Louisville. The train had a mile long load of box cars; they'd look for the ones with their doors open and no cargo. Riding the train in the winter was hard. One winter day it stopped because a passenger train was approaching and the freight train had to switch tracks. The passenger train used a protruding hook so it could come through and pick up the mailbag without stopping. When the freight train stopped, the brothers usually ran up and down the tracks to stay warm.

Depression boys riding the train

It was so cold that day that the conductor let the boys warm up around the stove he kept in the caboose. He promised to let them know before the train started moving again. To his last days, Earl was grateful for that kindness, which was unusual at the time since the train company did not encourage unofficial passengers. In fact, Earl had heard that people caught riding the trains in Texas were shot, so he was very thankful.

"When the weather broke, every week we'd ride that freight train on to Louisville," he said, "and many times the cars were full, so we had to ride where they hitched to each other." Sometimes, to sit, Earl had to straddle the train coupler or hitch: the constant shaking and jarring of the cars made his body ache. During warm weather, when they could find an empty car, usually after the train had dropped a load down South, they would ride with their feet hanging off the side and the wind blowing through their hair.

"We would ride going up and going back, and we'd get us enough money to last us the week. I remember riding up and seeing the movies *Shipmates Forever* and *Flirtation Walk* close to Jefferson Street. Carl and I rode that freight train several times. When it stopped for water that was our cue and we knew to get off."

One time Carl had gone to Louisville to pick up a tricycle for Ruth's son Charles, and Earl went to meet him. But that day the train didn't stop for water, so Earl watched Carl standing at the open door while waving and holding a tricycle as it went past around 45 miles per hour. The train stopped only six miles down the track, but that was far enough. "I was crying because when I saw him go by; I thought I had lost my brother," Earl explained laughing.

Earl remembered his brother, through a lot of practice, doing well in public speaking. Carl was quite skinny and trying to put on extra muscle at the time. "I remember Carl buying the Charles Atlas exercise manual through the mail. Atlas was the body builder of the time, and Carl would walk through the house exercising his arms up and down and practicing his speeches. He would practice the "Gettysburg Address" and the poem "Trees." Once I heard the words "four score and seven years ago," I knew he was at it again. I sure learned a lot about public speaking," Earl said, laughing.

The land on Carl's six-acre farm was difficult to cultivate for food. During the summer of 1935, the rest of the family (except for Jim W.) moved from Falls of Rough to Caneyville so they all could be together. Janie and her children rented a three-room house. They also had a cow, a calf, and Carl's pony. Earl and his brother were embarrassed by their family's poverty.

"It was a long 12 miles into Caneyville. It took about ten hours to get there with everything we had," Earl said. "We had decided to time it so we wouldn't go in during daylight. We kind of had a little pride and a little embarrassment, using a mule and a wagon along with leading a cow and calf. The cow was real skinny too. We weren't used to being embarrassed and we had to go right through Caneyville when we moved. We did it and I got 11 dollars later for that skinny cow when I sold it."

Earl got a pony of his own, which suffered from poor health. He tried to sell it for a price of 15 dollars. A man in town offered him half that, but Earl stayed insistent on receiving his asking price. The man told Earl the pony was in poor health and might die, and Earl should take his offer. Earl didn't know the man's intentions with his pony, and felt he was trying to skin him. Earl with boldness, told the man he would only take 15 dollars, and if the horse died, he would die as his. The pony did later die, but he was still Earl's.

Once at age 16, while living in Caneyville, Earl bought a club-footed mule for $7.50. It helped produce a good corn crop, and it was still there when he eventually left the farm. Earl usually had minimal access to an automobile; he mostly rode the mule, alongside his friend, Sol, who rode a bull calf when they courted girls. Earl and Sol, though, with their unusual means of transportation, never tried to take the girls out on a real date.

In Caneyville, Carl got involved in several activities, including theater, which was responsible for Earl getting yet another nickname. Carl played a character with a brother named "Prunes." For some reason the other kids picked up on that line, and for the rest of their time in Caneyville,

Earl was known as Prunes. The name stuck in the other towns where he would travel to play basketball.

"We had a schedule of traveling to Horse Branch, Beaver Dam, Central City, Hardinsburg, Leitchfield, and Short Creek to play our games," he said. "We played each team twice a year and some of those kids in those towns would even call me Prunes." Earl was sensitive about the name and what it implied, "It was desperate times then. I just didn't want people to think I got that name from standing in the food line and taking all the prunes the government may have given out."

Carl excelled in the classroom and outside of it and his younger brother looked up to him. "Carl was known as a hero to the local kids back in Louisville. When we swam in the Ohio, he was the only one that could swim out to Shippingport Island," Earl said. "He was a good swimmer and wasn't scared to dive off the sunken barges. Carl wasn't scared of anything and tough. He'd ride a bull and anything with four legs. We'd wrestle and roughhouse a lot growing up and it felt like a jackhammer when Carl hit you with one his bony hands. I saw him crush all his fingers in a car door on our way to a basketball game we were to play. He still played that night. Carl was patient too; he could fish all day with only a few nibbles. If I didn't get a nibble I'd be up skipping rocks in 10 minutes."

Carl graduated from Caneyville High School in 1936. He was an A student, so he didn't even have to take final exams. He went straight into the Navy.

"They called him to go to the Navy in May of '36," Earl said. "When he left, I cried for two to three weeks. I mean, I really lost it. Carl was a wonderful brother that stood by me, and we were good partners in everything we did. That wasn't just then, but it was the same throughout our life. So when I became so upset after he left, Mom sent me up to Allenville, Illinois, when I was 15 to stay with her brother Will and his two children Pearl and Jewell. I stayed up there all summer to settle down. I learned a lot about farming. They trusted me with things while there; looking back it makes me wonder that they did so much. I really don't think I knew what I was doing."

Carl (l.) and Bill (r.) in the Navy, 1937

CHAPTER EIGHT

DOWN TO THE NEW FARM

When Earl came back to Kentucky after about three months, the family was back living in Louisville. Because the Depression was so difficult, the Smith's moving, for the most part, was always makeshift and not planned.

Earl in ROTC uniform, 1936

In Louisville, it was just he, Nina, and his parents at home, a house at 5th and Kentucky Streets; his father had gotten a contracting job as a painter with the school board. Earl attended Male High School as a sophomore, and during that one year he joined the Reserve Officers Training Core, or ROTC.

Because the family had so little money, he actually joined for the uniforms, which he wore Monday through Thursday (wearing civilian clothes on Friday). His life might have been different if he continued attending school in Louisville, but a massive flood made that impossible.

The "1937 Flood" is legendary in and around Louisville. From Jan.13-24, the area received 15 inches of rain, and a total of 19 inches for the month. The Ohio River crested at 85.4 feet, (55 feet was regular flood stage), and 70 percent of the city was under water, leaving 175,000 people homeless. The devastation only added to the difficulties of living during the Great Depression.

The 1937 Louisville flood

"Mom, Nina, and I were trapped in this shot-gun house of ours behind Memorial Auditorium," Earl said. "My dad was working a regular job then and he was stuck there. There was this two-story house next door, and we went up there where the water was up to the mantels. There were no flood walls then, and the sewer system was all backed up. People were out just sitting in the water, floating in bath tubs. The Red Cross motorboats were going up and down 5th Street and never offered us anything. We never got a loaf of bread or nothing.

"Word comes out to break into the store down at the corner. There was looting for food going on. We were told to break in and get what we could. Water was coming up and down Kentucky (Street) so swift that you could hardly stand up. It was up to your waist. I didn't go to school during the flood, because you couldn't. Soon as the flood was over we had to go out to the farm and start over again. Dad said we would go down there until we got on our feet again. I think that was his favorite saying. He said it a lot."

Certain memories of events in Earl's life stood out to him. During the 1937 flood, Earl recalled a young girl across the street sitting on her front steps just watching as the water continued to rise. Towards his later years in life he would frequent a locally owned restaurant near his home. During one his visits, he began telling the story of the famous flood to the owner and he found that he was talking to that young girl. Once grown, she had moved to the area as well.

After the flood waters resided, Earl, Janie, and Nina went down to a new farm house that Carl had purchased in Falls of Rough; it was within walking distance from his initial six acres. Carl, later, sold the six acre property. The new land belonged to Lafe Allen, a local Methodist minister. Ministers were not paid well, and with the times so hard he couldn't pay the 24 dollar tax bill on the farm. Carl bought the deed before a foreclosure sale and he kept the property, only selling it before his death many years later.

Carl had an addition added and this house was a decent size compared to other houses in the area. It was 5 or 6 rooms with a 6 to 8 ft. front porch. From the dining room window you could look down a steep hill across Pleasant Run creek and onto the gravel highway that ran into the horizon.

The farm on Allen Hill was originally thought to be 100 acres, but turned out to be 67 acres. This farm's land seemed much better than the first he bought. It had an orchard, fenced garden, storm and storage cellar, and an old log barn. Janie was able to have her many signature rock-bordered flower beds and daffodils throughout the large yard.

The new house, 1937

Earl playing baseball on the new farm, 1937

The Depression had deepened. The family agreed that with what work Jim W. could get in Louisville, along with what they could grow in the garden and orchard, and bring home from hunting, they would have enough to eat. The house lacked electricity and running water, but there was a spring nearby neighbors called the "Everlasting Spring," meaning it never went dry.

"We'd put the milk and butter in a box underneath the spring to keep cold," Earl said. "It was about 100 feet away. We ate a lot of pork then to survive. We would eat meat just as quick as we got it and didn't need to put it underneath the spring."

At the new farm, Janie got some chickens to help out with the family income, but she couldn't afford to feed them. Earl had to break black walnuts and use the nuts as chicken feed. He took the chicken's eggs to a nearby store, where he'd get a nickel a dozen for them or trade for whatever staples the family needed. A loaf of bread was nine cents and a quart of milk was fourteen cents. Nobody had that kind of money, so bartering was common.

Bartering chicken and eggs for a new coat

Earl was back at Short Creek High School, a six-mile walk each way. He never enjoyed those long walks, and high school wasn't as easy for Earl as it had been for Carl.

"I always done well in math, made straight A's, but I could never figure out English," he said. "The adverbs and pronouns, I just couldn't understand."

Earl continued to play basketball at Short Creek after Carl graduated from Caneyville, playing on a dirt court. He always walked home after school and practice, often in the mud when it rained. He used the long walk home as an excuse to get out of running after practice. "I told my coach, I said, 'I got six miles to get home. Why don't you let me run as far as you can see me towards home, then I'll walk the rest of the way.' He thought that was sensible and he let me do that. I'd run in the direction with the most trees; I only had to do a good three blocks."

CHAPTER NINE

BEGINNING OF A NAVY CAREER

In December 1937, Earl decided he couldn't take anymore. He dropped out of school just after his 17th birthday and decided to join the service, as Bill and Carl had before him. Bill had joined the Navy in 1933, followed by Carl in 1936.

"My feet got cold from slopping through the mud to school," Earl said, "It was six miles to and from school every day. I told Momma, I said, 'I just can't take it.' She was against it."

He and Jim W. went down to the Navy recruitment office, in the Federal building at 7th and Broadway in Louisville. Jim W. had to sign for him because he was not yet 18. Like many men in those tough times, Earl enlisted partly for three meals a day. But as a saying at the time went, the armed forces were feeding them, but not needing them. It was difficult to get into the services at that time. As many as 50 men joined Earl to take the physical exam. In the end, only Earl and nine others were accepted. Earl found out boys weren't accepted that day for various reasons ranging from flat feet, to being uncircumcised, and even not having a trigger finger. Upon Earl's acceptance, his father tried to talk him out of it, to no avail.

"I enlisted three days after my birthday on Dec. 26, 1937, and they called me up early in March of 1938," Earl said. "When I left, my parents scraped together all the money they had. I had on a hand-me down suit from Carl and $3.42 when I got on the train. That was the start of my military life. My daddy cried, I'll never forget that. I couldn't remember him crying before." He said this as he lowered his head, covered his face, and began to sob. "I had to go. Everybody was at a standstill, just surviving then."

He continued: "I got my papers to report back to the Louisville 7th and Broadway Post Office. I kissed Mom and left, and didn't think about anything. I didn't have anything to miss other than my family, and my two brothers were already in and making money. That was the influence."

Earl in boot camp platoon photo, 1938

Enlisted men went to one of two places for 16 weeks of basic training (aka boot camp)—Great Lakes Naval Base in North Chicago, Illinois, or Hampton Roads Naval Base in Norfolk, Virginia, and Earl set off for Virginia.

When Earl stepped off the bus at Hampton Roads, his basic training experience began. A Chief Petty Officer began to torment him and scream, "Move it, move it! Move it, boot, move now! I ain't your mommy asking you! It's me! I'm telling you!" Earl was rushed inside, signed in, and then ordered to strip naked. His possessions and civilian clothes were boxed up and then sent back home. Earl, along with hundreds of other young men, shivering from being nude, waited in line to have their heads shaved. Then, the recruits, with their arms crossed and walking in an assembly-line fashion, received three vaccination shots to each arm; some passed out from the sight of the needles. Next, they received uniforms (with little attention to size), a hammock to sleep in, and a rifle. When they were issued a rifle, they were told, "You can't be a sailor until you hit the sea, so right now we're going to make a soldier out of you."

Basic training began at 5 a.m., and continued for ten hours with marching, over-your-head rifle drills, running, swimming, rowing, loading shells into a five-inch gun, and learning how to follow orders, mostly disagreeable ones. The day didn't stop until "Taps" was played, meaning lights out for bed. Earl admits being a little overwhelmed during his first week, but because of his ROTC experience, he eventually found boot camp easy, and it was not hard for him to pick up the military drills.

Earl's Platoon 16 consisted of 74 fellow recruits, and many razzed him, the guy everyone now called "Smitty," about being from Kentucky. They joked that the Navy put rocks in his shoes to get him on the train. Some said they were amazed that he didn't wear his shoes backwards.

Earl, just out of boot camp, 1938

Earl was also a hard worker and good with mechanical things. In basic training, he learned that he'd also picked up some of Carl's entrepreneurial spirit. One of a recruit's duties was to scrub his seabag and hammock once a week. Some were too lazy, so they paid Earl to do it for them.

Scrubbing by hand with a scrub brush and military issued

lye soap, he charged 15 cents for a seabag and ten cents for a hammock. When the group went on leave after boot camp, it wasn't unusual for them to lack money for a bus ticket home, but Earl earned an extra 80 dollars from his side business.

After completing basic training, some men would stay in Norfolk for an undetermined time. Those who stayed to wait for assignments would wander into town, which the locals frowned upon. Earl remembered signs in yards that read "Sailors and dogs keep off the grass."

Earl was excited to be a sailor. A recruit would get a ten day leave after basic, but a platoon could earn additional days. For example, a platoon could earn a star for tasks completed in competition against other platoons, with each star worth an extra day of leave. Earl and his platoon earned six extra days, 16 days of leave after basic training. He happily headed back home for a long leave along with a little extra money.

He saw amazing things during basic that he had never seen back home. At Newport News, VA, he witnessed the building of the USS *Enterprise,* a Navy carrier known as "The Big E." He was astounded by the size, more than 800 feet long and 143 feet tall, and with the carrying ability of 96 aircraft.

"That thing was something to see then," Earl recalled the memory, becoming excited again as he described that first time. "On leave, I went home and down to the Falls and bragged to everyone about what I had seen."

Earl remembered particularly his excitement in telling Uncle Maine about the Big E, and hearing him say, both zestfully and in genuine wonder, "My, my."

In boot camp, and four months following, with the rank of Apprentice Seaman, recruits earned 21 dollars a month (17 dollars after insurance was deducted). With the rank of Seaman Second Class and on to Seaman First Class, pay increased to 36 dollars. A Division Officer recommendation was then needed after a determined amount of time served. A sailor must pass a written exam for rank and pay promotion to petty officer.

"When it came to rank," Earl explained, "a Seaman Apprentice would have one stripe on the end of the sleeve, Seaman Second two stripes, and

Seaman First three stripes. These stripes could be red for engineering or white for seamanship, and these colors determined the division you were a part of. The Petty Officer now had what we called the crow or the white perched eagle on his upper arm and three levels of stripes. I started at the bottom, making the minimum and with one red stripe, but I was happy."

The perched crow or eagle was also known as the Chevron and a sailor would receive a hash mark on his cuff for every four years he served. Earl would initially have a red left cuff hash mark for being in the engineering department, then once a petty officer, he would have the symbolic crossed hammers emblem under the perched eagle for being a shipfitter.

Earl was feeling great about getting through basic training when he boarded his first ship, USS *Fanning DD-385,* a Mahan-Class Destroyer. Then he got sea sick for the entire 60-day transport.

"I was sick before I got out of Chesapeake Bay," Earl said. He told himself. "Oh, Smith, you done made a mistake."

"I was throwing up and dry heaving so much that when I got to Cuba, I planned to run away. So, we get to Gitmo (the U.S. Naval Base

Earl and friend in Honolulu photo booth, 1938

at Guantanamo Bay), and everything settled down because we were not moving. But when we got back on the ship, it was that old slow roll, that-a-way and this-a-way."

Some of the other sailors had fun at his expense. "A sailor will kid you. One guy said eat pickles. Man, I must have eaten about three gallons of pickles. Another guy said eat onions and raw potatoes. I did everything the old-timers told me. They said drink no water. I made it to Panama and I said, 'This is a long way from the States. I'm going to make it to San Diego and then I'm leaving.' I'm still eating those onions, potatoes, and pickles and everything they told me. Then I saw a drinking fountain, I said, 'I'm going to die anyway, and I might as well die with some liquid in me.'

All three bothers standing at Falls of Rough farm, circa 1938

"It was two days out of San Diego, and I went down on that drinking fountain. I started drinking and I started feeling better just for a little. Then I began heaving up liquid. I had the dry heaves again…all of that slow constant ship motion before was the reason why I was so sick. For some reason, after I drank some water and had those heaves, I was never sick again after that, for my Navy career. On that first trip, I was homesick some, but seasick a whole lot."

Chapter Ten

USS *ARGONNE*

The next ship for Earl was the USS *Argonne* AG-31 auxiliary ship, an assignment he eagerly pursued so he could reunite with his brother, Bill. Named for a famed World War I battle in the woods of northeastern France, the *Argonne* was the flagship (Admiral aboard) for the base force commander of the Pacific Fleet. The *Argonne* was in the Atlantic Ocean, amid German aggression, even before hostilities broke out in the Pacific.

Earl was always relieved when he returned to the United States and got away from the dangers of the Atlantic.

USS Argonne

The *Argonne*, docked in the Los Angeles Harbor in 1939, gave Earl the chance to spend time in L.A. and the surrounding area. He recalled once standing inside the Pacific Electric station, a mass transit system, and talking to the well-known actor George Murphy, who later was elected to United States Senate in 1964. They struck up a quick friendship and spent part of the day walking around, talking, and just hanging out. The time in L.A. also included an encounter with a Gypsy fortune teller, who grabbed Earl's arm and offered to read his palm and tell his fortune for 35 cents.

He agreed, and she told him four things that would occur throughout his life. He remembered them all clearly, and noted three ended up coming true: he would marry a redhead; never be rich, but not need anything; and he would be scammed by two men. The one that didn't bear out was she said he would live to the age of 93.

On the *Argonne*, for the first time, Earl crossed the equator, an imaginary line dividing the Earth into north and south hemispheres. The Navy had a time-honored tradition for first-timers, a ceremonial hazing, which was enacted just before crossing. Those being indoctrinated into this "mystery of the deep," were known as "pollywogs," inducted by those who had crossed before, the "shellbacks," a ceremony based around Roman mythological characters King Neptune (god of the sea), his queen Salacia, and the Royal Court.

Equator hazing with King Neptune's Royal Court (hangman in foreground), circa 1939

The shellbacks imitated these characters and initiated a series of hazing rituals meant to humiliate the pollywogs. The inductees might be forced to kiss the fish-oiled covered stomach of the royal baby, the fattest guy on the ship, or they might have to crawl through a 20 ft. nylon shoot filled with ketchup and mustard covered food scraps and smelling of garbage while the shellbacks lightly beat them with a mesh sling made up of wetted down rolls of canvas. Additional tricks included putting them on lookout for the equator or shaving their heads in an odd manner. Earl would cross the equator a total of 28 times, but he kept his hair, along with many fond memories of that first trip.

Earl worked in the *Argonne*'s sheet metal department, which maintained metal and plumbing. Bill was a Chief Petty Officer at the time, and eventually put in charge of the department and his little brother. Earl got yet another nickname, Butch, used only by his older brother Bill.

"When Bill was put as head of the department," Earl said, "he brought me over and said 'Butch, I'm not going to show any slack while you work with me just because you're my brother.' He never did, either, but I learned a lot from him. He taught a lot of what I know today. He was smart and could always pick up things quick."

Earl and Bill in the Virgin Islands

Once in the Navy, Bill was a tough fighter who was known to drink a little. He was single then, a little bowlegged, but a good dancer, and very well-known to the ladies. In 1939, Earl remembered being docked with Bill in the Virgin Islands on the *Argonne*. He was walking and saw a sailor getting tossed out of a bar during a fight with a couple of G.I.s, going back in and getting tossed out again. Then he realized it was Bill, and quickly approached him; Bill was now lying on his back. Earl, standing over him with concern, said, "Bill, you can't go back in there again, you won't make it out next time. You're coming with me!"

Later that year, while the brothers were still stationed on the *Argonne*, Bill was sent to the brig after putting a guy in the hospital during a fight in a civilian dance hall in San Pedro. Finding out about the fight, Bill's commanding officer responded, "Smith, is the U.S. Navy bigger than you or are you bigger than the U.S. Navy? You have thirty days to figure it out. You are a good fighter, but you need to save it for the Japanese." Bill was then dropped a rank for that fight. Earl never really asked about this incident; he just laughed and assumed Bill probably danced with somebody's girl.

"Bill was a dancer, and he could fight just as good as he could dance, too," Earl said. "Bill was rough and ready at all times." Nevertheless, Bill quickly regained his rank and continued to fulfill his military commitments with good character.

While on the *Argonne*, Earl and Bill were docked out on the West Coast. The ship had just been given orders to head to Norfolk, then up to the World's Fair in New York. Earl and Bill's plans instantly changed when they were notified their father had been involved in a terrible accident at home.

At Falls of Rough, Jim W. had come home from a hunting trip and sat the Remington pump rifle Carl had left behind against the wall. Janie moved it, but the safety wasn't on; Jim W. was hit in the back and the edge of his lung was pierced. He rushed to Marion's (Uncle Maine's) home for help. The main road was more than a quarter-mile away, and Maine quickly put Jim W. on his sled which was pulled by his two work mules, Nip and Tuck. They carried him to somewhere they could get help, presumable the nearby general store, and he was transported by car to the hospital in Louisville. He quickly recovered and returned home with the actual bullet in his hand as a token.

After the shooting, Earl and Bill got 10 days of emergency leave to spend time with their Dad, then they resumed orders and joined the *Argonne* in Norfolk.

Earl recalled events of 1939, before he was stationed at Pearl Harbor. "It was getting bad in Europe. I remember being back in Norfolk, after the accident with Dad, on the *Argonne* with Bill. We were getting ready to go up to New York for the World's Fair. I never even heard of the World's Fair at that time in my life, but was eager to go. We then received orders to return to the West Coast, because Hitler made accusations that the United States was preparing for war by having so many ships on the East Coast. I never understood fully the reason why we left, and why we left fast. We left so fast we left our captain, and he had to fly down and rejoin us at Gitmo. I knew our freighters were getting sunk by German submarines in the Atlantic before any declaration of war. We were in South Hampton, England, prior to the war and I could hear the buzz bombs being dropped by the Germans. They were starting to hit that place pretty hard. I had trouble figuring it out back then, as powerful as Germany was, you know, they weren't any bigger than Texas."

Janie and Jim W. at this time were able to maintain the house at Falls of Rough while also returning to Louisville to live when needed. For Christmas in 1939, Bill, Carl, and Earl returned to Louisville together. At the time, Carl hadn't seen his family in Kentucky for three years. Little did Earl know at the time, he would not see his family again until 1946.

As the brothers returned to the Los Angeles Harbor, they were involved in an automobile accident at 2 a.m. near Phoenix, Arizona. Bill's 1936 Ford rear-ended a cattle truck with no taillights and then slid under it with the truck bed crushing the car's wind-shield. Earl lost a lot of blood: a passerby found him lying on the side of the road. Earl recalled that the Good Samaritan had had both his legs amputated below the knees and walked on his leather padded stubs; he took Earl to the hospital in a modified Chevy truck.

"I always wished I could have thanked him for saving me, but I never got a chance," Earl said. "I was bad off, and here was a guy with no legs helping me."

Bill's injuries were more serious, and he went to another hospital. Carl was unhurt; he only had a torn pants leg. He stayed nearby to help care for his brothers. Bill ended up with 13 stitches in his head, while Earl, who broke his right orbital bone, received nine stitches above his eye.

Bill unloaded the car in Phoenix for 60 dollars, and they made the rest of the trip by bus. Earl got back an hour late and was considered absent without leave (AWOL); Bill, still on the *Argonne* with Earl, and Carl had days of leave remaining. Carl returned to Hawaii, where he was stationed.

Going AWOL, was considered a serious offense that could lead to court-martial. This was a military procedure that determines guilt in armed forces via jury and subject to military law. Earl spoke to his executive officer, who asked if he had paid for his medical bills. Earl told him he had, and the officer said that was sufficient punishment, but he still had to give him something. He sent Earl to the chain locker-room below the bow where the anchor was stored, where he spent six hours scraping loose paint, dirt, and rust off the 16-inch diameter links, then shining and repainting them.

By December 7, 1941, Earl was looking forward to getting out of the Navy. In September of that year, while on R and R in Los Angeles, he'd meet "The Rose," a local high school girl named Pearl (Penny) Silk. Penny was a pretty cheerleader from a local middle class family; her father was a welder and her mother was a housewife. Earl initially had been interested in one of Penny's friends, but once he saw Penny, he was instantly smitten.

Earl's friend introduced him as Snuffy Smith after a character from the 1934 comic strip "Barney Google," and that's how she referred to him from then on. They corresponded through letters, and now he wanted to spend more time with her. Penny was also falling for the young Earl, and he was only two weeks from discharge, with visions of getting home for Christmas.

"I'd been there for 20 months," he said, and "the newness had worn off. I didn't care anything about Hawaii at all. When I was there, we got American music only 30 minutes a day and that was from 12 to 12:30. The songs were from "Singin' Sam, the Coca-Cola Man." That's all the American music we got. We got sick of the Hawaiian music.

"We were kind of bitter, in a way, that we were out there doing nothing. In Europe, Hitler had been feeding this thing all along, easing up to it since 1939. And here we are sitting out here like that. President Roosevelt had to know something."

Bill had been transferred off the *Argonne* in the fall of 1940. All that remained for Earl was to catch a ride on a transport ship to return to Hawaii from San Francisco and then pick a new group and return to the West Coast again. Earl was scheduled to be on that ship, and he had visions of hitting the coast, and spending time with Penny before returning to Louisville. Little did he realize what was about to happen, and that he would not see his parents and sisters again for six years.

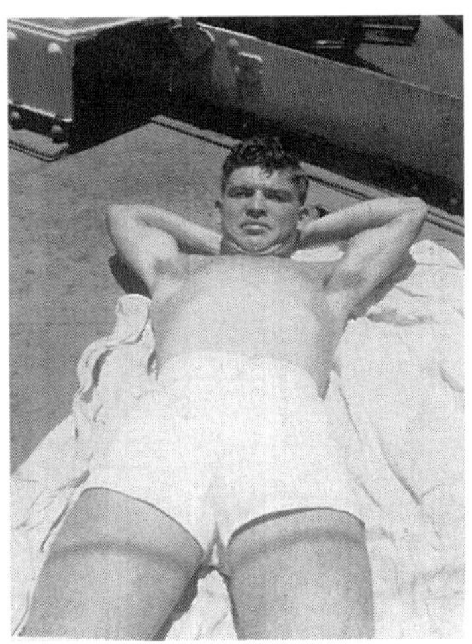

Earl relaxing on the USS Argonne *at Pearl Harbor during the late fall, 1941*

Earl and shipmate on USS Argonne *at Pearl Harbor, late fall, 1941*

Chapter Eleven

BUILD-UP

Pearl Harbor, a lagoon located on the southern coast of the Hawaiian Island of Oahu, was called "Wai Momi" (Water of Pearl) by the Hawaiians because of its many pearl-producing oysters. The U.S. Navy has always had interests there, and in the late 1800s, the Reciprocity Treaty was signed between the United States and the Kingdom of Hawaii, under which the United States obtained exclusive rights to Pearl Harbor as part of the agreement to allow Hawaiian sugar to enter U.S. ports duty free. Later, a group of American and English businessmen who had settled there overthrew the Hawaiian monarchy, and Hawaii was eventually annexed by the United States before the turn of the century. Pearl Harbor, with its ten square miles of navigable water, soon developed into a major strategic port for the U.S. military.

During the early part of the 20th century, Japan was one of the five permanent members of the council of the League of Nations, an international organization which was founded after WWI and whose principal mission was to maintain world peace.

Nonetheless, tensions had been building between the U.S. and Japan for some time. Japan's military began expanding into Asia and the Pacific Ocean, and, in 1936, they allied with Nazi Germany. The expansion created an all-out war with China, beginning in 1937. The same year, Italy joined to form the Axis alliance. At its peak, the Empire of Japan had the ninth strongest economy and third largest naval fleet in the world.

In 1941, after moving from San Diego, most of the U.S. Navy Pacific Fleet was docked at Pearl Harbor. In response to Japanese aggression, the United States and Great Britain imposed an oil embargo and demanded that Japan withdraw from China. Japan saw itself with two options, either to withdraw from China or attempt to cripple the U.S. military, seizing control over the oil, and continuing their advancement into Asia. Still, in early December of that same year, the United States and Japan were involved in heavy negotiations over the matter.

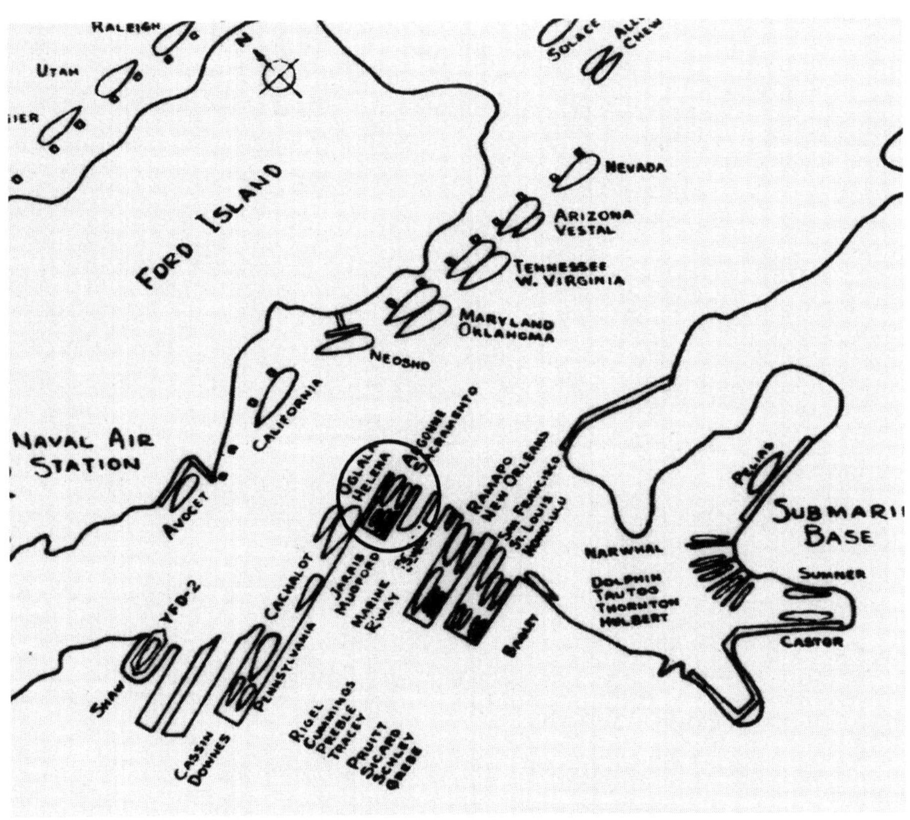

Map of battleship positions at Pearl Harbor
Earl's ship, the USS Argonne, *at the Ten-Ten dock is circled*

CHAPTER TWELVE

ATTACK ON PEARL HARBOR

Group of Japanese fighter planes ready for takeoff from carrier

On December 7, 1941, six Japanese Navy carriers with 423 planes sat in choppy waters, 235 miles north of Hawaii. As the carriers pitched and rolled, waves crashed across the flight decks. Crewmen clinched themselves to the aircraft to keep them from going over the side. Then the carriers turned into the wind, and at 6:10 a.m. the first attack wave of 183 planes roared into the sky toward the Island of Oahu. Pilots reconfirmed their navigation target by using a Honolulu radio station's music

Torpedo bomber taking off while Japanese sailors wave and yell, "Bonzii"

as a guiding beam through dense clouds, wondering if the harbor would even be visible. Then the clouds broke, and they saw a long white line of coast, Oahu's most northern point, with Pearl Harbor in the far distance.

At 7:50 a.m., a light training plane from the USS *Argonne*, performing training exercises over the island of Oahu's North Shore, was attacked and shot down by two planes. The pilot, before parachuting, was able to radio home the make and visible markings seen on the enemy planes, as German made, with distinguished "Red Suns," on their wingtips. These two planes, and with many others to follow, then headed straight for Pearl Harbor, the air fields at Hickam and Wheeler, Ford Island, and Kaneohe and Ewa Field.

Most of the enlisted men were asleep when the first wave of planes hit at 7:55 a.m. It was a Sunday, the only day they were allowed to sleep late. A large plane formation was initially detected by the newly installed naval radar, but were shrugged off as a group of U.S. B-17 Fortress bombers which were returning from a 14 hour flight from California and expected that morning. The Japanese planes came like a swarm of bees into the harbor. More than 180 enemy aircraft engaged in the first wave. Japanese planes were initially unseen until they were right up on the Americans. They flew out of the bright morning sun to avoid detection. Also, some flew low and undetected through the Waianae Mountain notch, KoleKole Pass, and over a volcanic ridgeline, Diamond Head.

Seconds after the attack began, the general quarters' bell rang, signaling the sailors to man their battle stations. "General Quarters, General Quarters, This Is Not A Drill, This Is Not A Drill, All Hands Man Your Battle Stations!" When Earl, heard the alarm sound, he headed for his locker two decks up, above his sleeping quarters, next to the metal shop where he worked. He could hear sailors' Navy-issued wooden clogs clicking on the ship's floor as the men scrambled to their posts. As he put on his shoes, Earl looked out a small porthole above his locker and saw Ford Island, a Navy base and airfield, and battleship row.

"We were relaxed because it was peace time," he recalled, "but as I looked out the porthole I saw a plane fly by, real low, that I didn't recognize. We didn't know what the Japanese Rising Sun insignia was; I knew nothing about the Rising Sun. I saw this plane go off and I saw the big red fireball on it. I didn't know who we were about to be at war with; nine sailors out of ten would of said the same thing."

He continued: "My buddy next to me who didn't have access to a porthole said, 'We are having maneuvers early on a Sunday morning.' I said, 'Maneuvers, hell. This is the real thing. It is not even eight o'clock.' Right when I said that, I saw a hangar on Ford Island blow up; that was when I knew we were at war. We were both stunned on what was happening."

During the early moments of the attack, some sailors would scream, "Who's bombing us?" Other sailors found out in other ways. "I even recall of being told later of a boy being killed in the mess hall when they attacked," Earl said. "A bullet went through the side of the ship just like a drill. He was standing there talking to a guy, and the bullet went right through his heart."

Earl's battle station was three decks up; he was a loader on an anti-aircraft gun. "When I got up to my battle station, there was a plane strafing cars that were parked along the dock," Earl said. "Most of the cars belonged to officers. It was a well-planned attack. There were so many of them (planes), it was amazing they didn't run into each other. They were just all over us."

From their high advantage point, Earl and his buddies had a front row seat to most of the destruction. The planes strafed everything down

Photo taken from Japanese plane during the attack. The large smoke column in center is Battleship Row. The smaller column to the left is Ten-Ten Dock

A view down Ten-Ten dock

Main Street in Honolulu, along with cars returning to the harbor. Many officers were being hurriedly driven by their wives to be dropped off. Also, they targeted the barracks at Hickam Airfield. The block structure building, No.1102, still holds bullet holes and blown out pieces of concrete as a reminder of this attack. The men saw motor launches loaded with sailors being strafed with bullets as they tried to reach the ships to help. To add to the turmoil, the 12 B-17 Fortress bombers expected in that morning, unaware of the ongoing attack, attempted to land at 8:00 a.m. Because they were unarmed—to save weight—they could only dodge Japanese fighters and U.S. anti-aircraft fire. Most managed to land intact, with one landing on a golf course. Next to the *Argonne*, the minelayer USS *Oglala* was heavily damaged by the concussion from a single Japanese torpedo that hit the USS *Helena*. A torpedo went under the *Oglala* and slammed into the *Helena* killing 22 men. The *Oglala* rolled on its side, causing the mast to hit the *Argonne*.

"The *Oglala* was tied to the light cruiser *Helena* and was able to be moved immediately following being hit," Earl recalled. "We did this so the *Helena* would not be pinned in behind the *Oglala* and against the dock. She [the *Helena*] attempted making it out of the port. We were all bottled in. The entrance into Pearl Harbor is so narrow that ships can't pass each other there. Almost the whole West Coast Fleet was at Pearl Harbor. The planes came down over a mountain and they would be on top of us before we could even take aim at them. And we couldn't shoot in all directions. A lot of ships had other tall ships tied on the outside of them, blocking their ability to shoot. We certainly didn't have much time to think, but most of us realized we were at the point of no return. We were at war with the Japanese."

Sailors had two responsibilities, their military duty and their special duty. Earl worked in the metal shop; that was his special duty. Militarily, he was expected to load a .50-caliber machine gun. Because everything happened so quickly, locks on the ammunition boxes had to be shot off and most of the crew wore neither a helmet nor a flak jacket. Earl soon found that his fellow shipmates maintaining the .50-caliber gun were inexperienced. In the chaos, Earl recalled them turning the gun toward a Japanese plane and accidentally shooting the *Argonne*'s mast. Even during

Pier 16 and the Hammerhead crane, with Ten-Ten just to right

the mayhem, the *Argonne* was still able to shoot down a Japanese bomber plane with her .50-caliber artillery. Once hit, the plane turned and crashed near Ford Island.

On that fateful day, the *Argonne* lay in the first repair slip at the Ten-Ten Dock, where it was partly shielded from the enemy planes by a huge crane used to lift parts and equipment at pier 16. Ten-Ten, the first dock of the Navy yard, was an unloading zone for the wounded because it was the closest dock to the Navy hospital. The *Argonne* took machine gun fire, but no bombs. She attempted to defend herself against the assaulting aircraft by firing the 3-and 5-inch guns along with small caliber arms. After the attack, a rumor circulated among sailors that the Japanese did not want to damage the crane, they called it the "hammerhead," the biggest floating crane in the Pacific, because it would be useful later if they took the harbor. But Earl knew none of this when he made his way up three decks towards his gun.

"We were shooting in less than five minutes, and from then on it was just turmoil," he remembered. "They [the Japanese] were after the battleships first. We could see torpedoes breaking through the surface of the water. We could see them dropped. After a few explosions there were sailors in the water; we had boats going over assisting the battleships. There were boys burned to charcoal under their helmets still leaning on their anti-aircraft guns. They were just charcoal. . . . It was boom boom, fire and everything. Planes were hitting the water. Sailors were jumping off the ships in the burning water trying to swim. Some of them slick with oil, trying to swim."

He continued: "I had a ringside seat. I could see 360 degrees, up and down in the water. I quickly learned wood was worse in many ways than shrapnel, because of the splintering decks I saw piercing sailors."

Japanese naval officer standing by scoreboard as first wave of planes return

The battleships were lined up in rows, tied two by two, side by side, near Ford Island. Earl saw the USS *Oklahoma* roll over in the water; as its sailors abandoned ship, he watched the Japanese strafing them from the air. He saw the USS *Arizona* blow up, thrown into the air, splitting in half and sending bodies all over the harbor. By igniting a million pounds of gunpowder, the explosion touched off fierce fires that burned for two days. The USS *Nevada* tried to make it out of the harbor as it steamed past the Ten-Ten Dock at 9:50, but Earl saw a bomb go down its smokestack, causing it to explode as well. The *Nevada* was hit with five bombs during the first attack. The Japanese intended to sink the *Nevada* with hopes of blocking the channel out of the harbor. By this time everything was either blown up, burning, or smoldering. All that could be seen of Ford Island aircraft station was dense smoke.

"The *St. Louis* made it out of the harbor," Earl said, "A Japanese plane went by so close and level with us I could have hit it with a rock, I believe if I had one. This pilot waved smiling and laughing. I could see him. He was that close. I could see his goggles and what he looked like. This was

The forward magazine of the USS Shaw *exploding, with USS* Nevada *burning on left*

on the first wave (attack). I then saw that pilot crash into the dry dock where the *Pennsylvania* was being repaired."

The second wave came about 9:55 a.m. and included another 170 Japanese planes. "These Japanese planes seemed to be mostly torpedo planes compared to the fighters and bombers I had seen with the first wave," Earl said. By then, the U.S. Navy had search and rescue ships looking for survivors from the first attack. American ships could not use their big guns for fear of hitting some of their own troops in the water. "We were so low on the water," Earl said. "It was a danger to your own ships and the sailors. We couldn't shoot those guns in the harbor. When using 8-inch guns, you can't shoot straight, and you must shoot at an angle with a second delay between each gun firing, or you will buckle the ship. You couldn't stand too close to these guns either, or they would tear your clothes off."

Sailor watches from Ford Island as USS Shaw *explodes*

Earl watched as the USS *Shaw* was blown in half in a volcanic plume of fire and smoke. Pieces of the ship were seen raining-down over a half mile away. He saw the burning oil and bodies and black smoke blotting out the sky. Dive bombers and torpedo bombers flitted overhead unleashing a flurry of bombs and launching torpedoes into water. Earl could see the torpedoes' wake as they headed toward the remaining craft along battleship row. Although chaotic to the Americans, the attack was well synchronized by the Japanese; once the planes dropped their bombs and torpedoes, they quickly returned back to the Navy carriers. Once the returning planes arrived, the carriers turned toward home.

Marine in grief with hands over head

Earl saw one saving grace for the Americans: All but one of their carriers had been out to sea. The USS *Saratoga* and her sister ship, the USS *Lexington,* along with the USS *Enterprise,* had been prime targets of the attack, but they were not there. The *Saratoga* was in Puget Sound for an overhaul; the *Lexington* had left Pearl Harbor two days earlier to deliver scout bombers to Midway Island; and the *Enterprise* had been out delivering fighter planes to Wake Island and had been due back that day.

At the time of the attack on Pearl Harbor, his brother Bill was on the USS *Louisville,* a day out from Manila, Philippines. The Japanese invaded the Philippines on Dec. 8th; that was just ten hours after the Pearl Harbor attack because of the automatic time addition once crossing the international dateline. Because the Japanese took control of Borneo, where the *Louisville* normally refueled, the ship had only a few hours of fuel left.

"We still had a lot of firepower, anti-aircraft," Earl said. "The battleships, the ones on the ground didn't take a lot of torpedoes; they could still fire. I think they were surprised at how quickly and heavily we were able to fire back. The water wasn't deep in some areas and some ships were still shooting even though they were in the water sunk."

USS Arizona *burning after it exploded*

Ten-Ten Dock with USS Argonne *visible and USS* Oglala *capsized in front*

USS Cassin *with USS* Argonne *visible in the distance, within the smoke*

Wrecked destroyers USS Cassin *on right, with USS* Downes *and USS* Pennsylvania *astern (Ten-Ten Dock far right)*

When it was over, from the ships and airfields came the wounded—some horribly burned, others riddled by bullets and shrapnel. Military and civilian trucks were transformed into ambulances and hearses. Many of the harbor's wounded and dead were loaded at the Ten-Ten dock. At some hospitals, causalities were laid out on lawns while medics converted barracks, dining halls, and schools into temporary hospitals. For the many severely wounded and dying, nurses could only give morphine to help. They put a lipstick M on their foreheads to indicate the painkilling drug.

It had taken the Japanese about 90 minutes to kill more than 2,351 Navy, Army, and Marine personnel along with 49 civilians. Another 1,368 were wounded. Of 195 Pacific Fleet vessels present, 18 ships were damaged or sunk and repaired, and the Japanese destroyed 188 Navy and Army aircraft.

Those are the historical records, but Earl found the numbers questionable. As he recalled it, more ships were present during the attack, and the dead and wounded numbers didn't fully account for everyone. The battleships *Oklahoma, Nevada, California, Arizona* and *West Virginia* were destroyed along with the minelayer *Oglala,* and the cruisers *Helena*, *Honolulu*, and *Raleigh* took heavy damage. The destroyers *Cassin, Downes,* and *Shaw* were destroyed, and the *Helm* suffered moderate damage. The battleship *Nevada* was towed by a tug after being hit and beached off the Waipio Peninsula before it sank. The *Oklahoma* took seven torpedoes and capsized. Earl recalled it lying in the water with the propeller protruding. The ship was deemed unsalvageable and wasn't brought upright until March 1943, when 400 bodies were recovered.

The *Arizona* was the most heavily damaged. It sank in nine minutes after a bomb hit the ammunition magazines and destroyed the forward section of the ship taking 1,177 lives. The unsalvageable ship remains on the bottom of the harbor where it still entombs 900 sailors and Marines. More than 70 years later, its fuel oil still can be seen seeping out from its hull and floating above. Survivors from the crew say the oil will continue to leak until the last survivor dies.

It turns out the Japanese erred in their strategy because they didn't destroy the oil tankers, power station, and the Navy yard. With an untouched repair yard and continued electricity, ship repairs were even capable at night. Once repaired, they were able to be refueled and sent back into action. Also, the Japanese made a mistake by attacking in the harbor, which had much shallower water than the open sea. Although listed as destroyed, all but the two battleships and the *Utah,* an ex-battleship turned training ship, returned to war. These ships were deemed lost. The *Utah* was hit by two torpedoes during the opening moments of the attack and the ship capsized. To this day she still lies on her side and entombs 40 sailors.

Dead sailor in water

Asked whether he and his shipmates were scared, Earl said, "Everything happened so quick, we didn't have time to get scared. We were too stunned. We did have a guy that was in the sick bay during the attack who lost it. He ran down two decks, across the gangway and was later found in the Navy yard. All in all, we just did our jobs, performed our military duties."

He continued: "But even when I was afraid, I never thought of myself dying. I never pictured myself in the water drowned or shot and killed. I was scared a lot of times, but I never saw myself dying." What Earl didn't realize at the time, was that everything he experienced that day would haunt him for the rest of his life.

Immediately, rumors circulated, that the Japanese would next attempt a land invasion, and G.I.s stayed on alert until that afternoon. Then, another rumor began circulating that they were already on the island. That night, sailors slept in their uniforms and that continued for a month, anticipating another attack. As the sky was dark and silent around nine p.m., bombers from the carrier *Enterprise* flew over Pearl Harbor; they had been part of a strike group searching for the carriers that launched the Japanese raid.

Shot-up civilian car, with dead driver and passengers, killed eight miles from Pearl Harbor, in residential district

Earl described the resulting firestorm as "like Chicago on the Fourth of July," as the gunners began unloading without realizing they were firing on U.S. planes. The planes were not using running lights as a recognition symbol for U.S. aircraft. Three pilots were killed crashing into the harbor, and, one .50-caliber bullet fired from the direction of Ford Island penetrated the *Argonne*'s port side, killing two seamen.

"When we heard that report, we all started firing again," Earl said. "Mistakes like that happened a lot during that time. We all had fear that night. Later that night my knees began to knock uncontrollably. I couldn't stop them from shaking. It turned out to be nothing, but I couldn't stop shaking. That was scary, what had happened, but evidently there was no enemy out there then.

"A week later, I stood top side watching the *Arizona* still burning and hoping it was a dream, thinking maybe it was," Earl said. "Then I saw old-time sailors with years of service, standing there crying like babies. It was really happening."

The following day, Dec. 8, President Roosevelt declared war on Japan. In a speech that rang loud in the ears of every American and united the country, FDR declared "Dec. 7, 1941, a date which will live in infamy." And he said, "No matter how long it may take us to overcome this premeditated invasion, the American people, in their righteous might, will win through to absolute victory."

After things settled down, everyone began salvaging. Like most, Earl helped retrieve bodies and remains from the harbor, which had taken on a horrible odor. Bodies had to be identified first, a difficult task because so few were wearing dog tags that morning and some men were badly disfigured. The dead were buried in quickly-dug graves on the rim of the harbor and in Punchbowl Cemetery, located in an area of Honolulu that in ancient times was known as the hill of sacrifice. Earl was on salvage duty for three months, helping in raising ships and attempting to repair, and get them back into operation, until his eagerly-requested transfer to his brother's ship was granted.

Building 1102

Marine squad firing volleys over coffins of 15 officers and men killed on Dec. 7, 1941

Before his transfer, Earl heard rumors—later confirmed—about sailors trapped underwater in airtight compartments, who had banged on the side of the ship for days after the attack. The Navy acknowledged there was no way to find or reach the men without endangering many others. Three sailors were found in such a compartment on the USS *West Virginia*. There was a calendar on the wall with 16 days marked off.

The *Argonne* crew was later cited for their quick response and bravery during the attack. Commander F. W. O'Connor, her commanding officer, said the crew "performed their duties in accordance with the best traditions of the service in helping to get wounded men from damaged ships, recover bodies from the water, and assisting with repair facilities to full capacity."

The *Argonne* received a Battle Star for its service at Pearl Harbor. After the war ended, the *Argonne* transported troops home from the western Pacific before the Navy decommissioned her in 1946.

As the war escalated, many American families, including the Smiths, showed support for their sons off fighting. Pictured: Jim W., Janie, Nina, and Ruth.

CHAPTER THIRTEEN

BEHIND THE SCENES

The Japanese attack on Pearl Harbor was intended as a preventive measure to keep the United States Pacific fleet out of the war that Japan planned in Southeast Asia, Great Britain, the Netherlands and the United States in the Philippines. Japan hoped to neutralize the entire fleet and, more importantly, knock out the aircraft carriers.

Japan's governmental and military decisions were being made by Emperor Hiroshito and Hideki Tojo who had become prime minister just two months earlier. Americans later blamed him for the attack, and he was eventually executed by hanging for war crimes, but the Emperor was never prosecuted. Admiral Isoruko Yamamoto, Commander-in-Chief for the Japanese Imperial Navy, who planned and trained those involved in the attack, had been educated in the United States. He had lived in the U.S. for four years while he pursued an English degree at Harvard and worked as a Naval Attache in Washington, D.C., during which he was also a senior officer in the Japanese military.

The U.S. and Japan were in negotiations and Yamamoto had a different view compared to Japan's leaders. He originally stipulated the attack should not begin until 30 minutes after Japan informed the United States that negotiations had ended; the attack took place before any declaration of war was made by Japan. Two waves of attack were sent; a third wave of horizontal bombers flew high above the harbor, but with the dense smoke, visibility was too poor to precisely locate their targets.

The attack was a major success for the Japanese, but on a diary recording that was discovered after the attack, Yamamoto reportedly said, "I fear all we have done is to awaken a sleeping giant and fill him with terrible resolve."

Admiral Chester W. Nimitz was promoted to admiral of the Pacific Fleet on Dec. 17, 1941, taking the reins from Vice Admiral William S. Pye, who'd been given temporary command after the attack. Earl was already familiar with Admiral Nimitz from his time as commander of the *Argonne*, and he held him in high esteem. (Nimitz took over for Admiral Husband E. Kimmel, a Kentucky native, who was reduced to Rear Admiral after the bombing at Pearl Harbor.)

One Nimitz quotation, now on the monument at the World War II Memorial, Pacific Theater in Washington, D.C., demonstrated his strong personal feelings about the attack. "They fought together as brothers-in-arms. They died together and now they sleep side by side. To them we have a solemn obligation."

Chapter Fourteen

USS *LOUISVILLE*: TOGETHER AGAIN

USS Louisville

After the salvage cleanup at Pearl Harbor, and with a hard luck story to go along with his earlier transfer request, Earl convinced his commander to transfer him to the USS *Louisville* CA-28. The ship was a Northampton-Class heavy cruiser, where Bill was serving. Once again, Bill was Earl's boss.

Bill and Earl hadn't seen each other since April 1940, and both had lost touch. To join the *Louisville,* Earl had traveled from the East Coast to the West Coast between commissions. While in Long Beach, Earl spotted his brother leaving a local dance hall. Excited to see him, Earl approached Bill suddenly and grabbed his arm. Bill began drawing his fist back before he realized it was Earl. It became a pleasant reunion after that initial reintroduction.

Also, between commissions, Earl took Penny to Las Vegas and married her on April 6, 1942. She settled in Vallejo, CA, to finish high school, and he joined the *Louisville.*

Earlier in 1941, Bill and the *Louisville* had transported 148 million dollars worth of British gold from Simonstown or (Simon's Town), South Africa, to New York. British ships had been unable to do it because they were at war in Europe. The United States was considered neutral which allowed for safe transport. The *Louisville* would highlight the American flag while out in waters being patrolled by German U-boat submarines. Germany had the largest submarine fleet in the world, and was effective at destroying allied shipping. One incident was the sinking of the British cargo ship SS *Gairsoppa,* on February 17, 1941, off the western coast of Ireland. The *Gairsoppa* had been en route from Calcutta, India, to London, but instead went to the ocean floor carrying seven million ounces of silver, worth more than 210 million dollars today.

Serving together again, 1942

While the brothers were serving together, Bill gave Earl a few scares, and Earl recalled one in particular. Bill gave orders for Earl to drop anchor on the ship, something the younger brother had never done. The anchors were massive with some weighing up to 50,000 pounds and they shot out at projectile speed. Earl was terrified of damaging the ship and getting a court-martial.

"I asked one of the guys, 'What do you do?' He said you just pull that brake, hoping the brake stops it. He said if a certain color comes out, I think it was yellow, you want to run because the brake didn't stop it and the chain and everything is coming out. You're going to lose it all and take me with it. That's all I thought of."

Fortunately, the Chief Boatswain's Mate, who was in charge of the deck, knew the exact depth of the water and told Earl when to apply the brake. Earl managed to cut the brake just right, but not without a lot of sweating.

During this time, Bill met his future wife Raye Lukton in Oakland, CA. She had moved to California with her mother and oldest sister after turning 18. Raye was born to Russian Jewish immigrants in Denver, Colorado. Her mother was a former seamstress to the Czarina, Alexandra, wife of the last Russian Czar Nicholas II. (Nicholas II and his family along with three servants were executed during the Russian revolution in 1918.) Raye's mother worked to save enough money to immigrate to the U.S with her husband.

Raye was out on a date and Bill, ever the opportunist, casually approached her when her date went to the bathroom. He learned she was in mechanic's school because, with the demands of the war and with men off fighting, women were needed to supply the troops. Bill told her he was an airline mechanic and would help her study. He quickly got her phone number before her date returned.

Bill and Raye

She wrote it on a napkin, along with the promise of a date on one condition: he could not call her on Mondays because she would be doing her hair.

Bill and Raye dated for 28 days, then married in May, 1942, just weeks after Earl married Penny. They eventually settled in San Diego, California, with their children Janice and Steve, where later in life, Bill and Raye worked in selling, building, renting, and remodeling houses. They remained married until their deaths.

In the fall of 1942, Bill received his commission as a Chief Warrant Officer. Because the Navy realized it might cause resentment when a former peer becomes a supervisor, newly commissioned officers are moved, and so Bill left the *Louisville* for the heavy cruiser USS *Minneapolis,* where he had been when the ship was first commissioned on May 19, 1934.

The U.S. Navy was in a series of battles against the Imperial Japanese Navy in the South Pacific, during what was called the Guadalcanal Campaign, situated around Guadalcanal Island in the Solomon Islands chain.

Bill trained as a deep sea diver and underwater welder; Earl recalled his brother was one of the first sailors to weld aluminum. For awhile after the war, he taught metallurgy, (the study of physical and chemical behavior of metallic elements) at the Naval Training Center in San Diego. Bill's welding skills would become important.

Shortly after he left the Louisville, on Nov. 30, 1942, during the nighttime Battle of Tassafaronga near the Tassafaronga region on Guadalcanal, the *Minneapolis* had its bow blown off by two torpedoes. The crew successfully camouflaged her with palm branches and shrubs and she sailed into Tulagi of the Solomon Islands for temporary repairs. Earl saw Bill in Tulagi after the Minneapolis landed for repairs.

"The Minneapolis was hit pretty hard out there. I ran into him afterwards and we talked a little about it. He was a little shook up, but nothing ever really fazed Bill," Earl said.

USS Minneapolis *in Tulagi with blown bow after Battle of Tassafaronga, 1942*

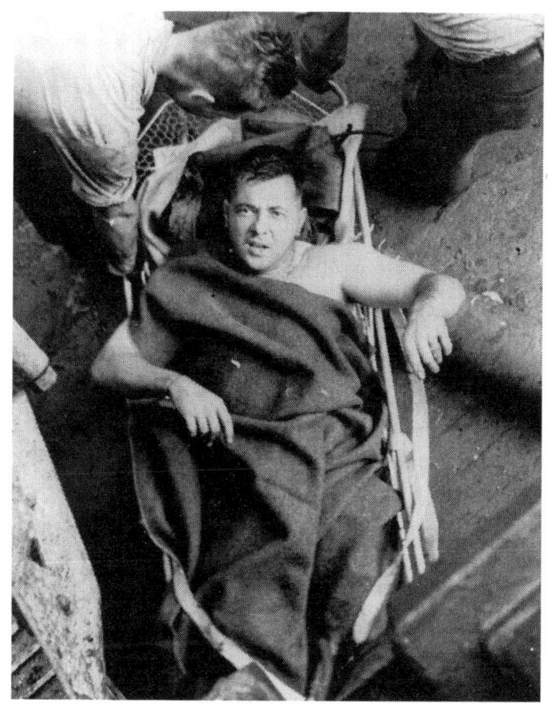

Bill's shipmate on stretcher after Battle of Tassafaronga

CHAPTER FIFTEEN

THE *LOUISVILLE* IN PURSUIT

The Japanese had landed on the Aleutian Islands, a chain of more than 300 small volcanic islands, 6,821 square miles of the Aleutian Arc that belonged to Alaska. The strategically located islands were coveted, because the holder of them controlled the Pacific routes. The Japanese reasoned that gaining control would prevent the United States from attacking across the Northern Pacific. Similarly, the United States feared the Japanese would launch aerial assaults on the West Coast of the United States.

Earl and "Lady Lou" maintenance crew, 1943

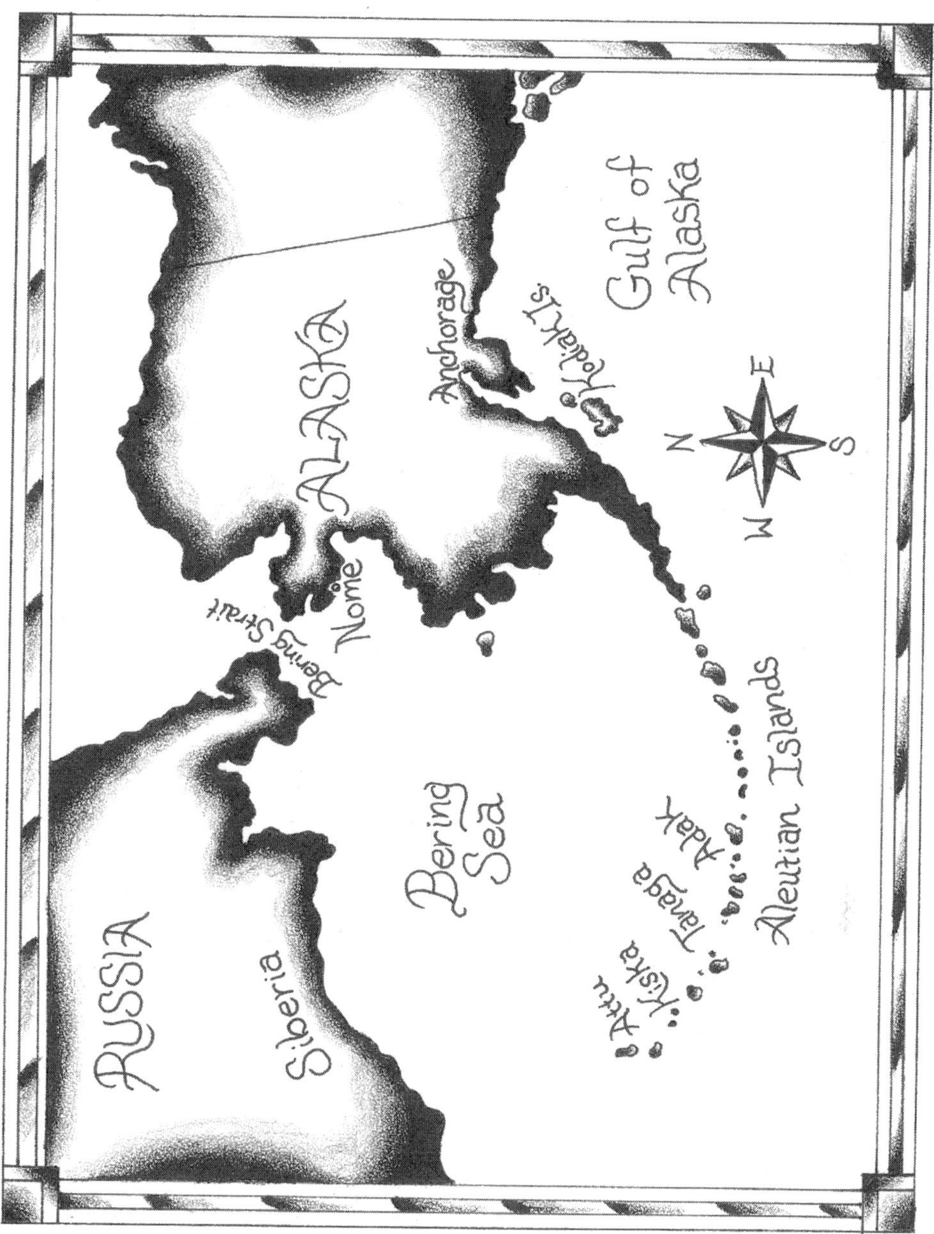

The *Louisville* patrolled near the Aleutians and in the Bering Strait for six months, with occasional short side trips to Siberia every few days. Sailing past Nome, Alaska, Earl recalled seeing Eskimos surrounded by igloos and sled dogs. Kodiak Island was a volcanic peak 30 miles off the southern coast of Alaska in the Gulf of Alaska. The Americans used the island for supply stops and as a major staging area for the North Pacific operation. The *Louisville* stopped periodically to pick up ammunition for ship battle and island bombardment. It was the only time Earl touched land for two years. Most of the places they were near were either jungle or full of enemy soldiers, and he felt no need to leave the ship.

"We'd stay out 120 days at a time and we had to stay moving. We couldn't get under 18 knots [a knot equals one nautical mile per hour, which typically equates to 1.15 miles per hour]," Earl said. "We transferred and brought on sailors and supplies with other ships, and the oil tankers would come up right beside us. The oil was straight crude oil, not refined. We did all this while we were still were moving out at sea. We would use a bolster chair, rope, and a pulley when transferring sailors. We sometimes changed captains and transferred the sick and injured that way just using a stretcher.

USS Louisville *transferring medical supplies from ship to ship*

"We once transferred beer onto a barge with use of a cargo net after picking it up in New Zealand," Earl said. "The *Louisville* didn't get one can; it was for the troops on land fighting. It was only beer, but it was heavily guarded."

Many people who were familiar with the ship called it the "Lady Lou" or the "Grey Ghost of the China Coast." Her bow was painted white to deceive submarines, with the rest painted several times with grey, black, and white. The Japanese submarines typically tried to gauge speed by judging the water spray coming a ship's bow, and the paint scheme was intended to make that difficult.

During the early part of June 1942, the *Louisville* provided cover fire so the marines could land in the Aleutians, and prevented the Japanese from getting reinforcements, but bad weather and challenging terrain created a back-and-forth battle that lasted more than a year. "The Japanese just out done us," Earl said. "We didn't capture anyone, or sink any major ship. They dug in like rats, and we thought they left, so they ordered us back down to the South Pacific. We did manage to sink seven freighters with the use of our scout planes while in the middle of the islands.

"When we sunk those ships," Earl continued, "we were shooting over a mountain, with the scout planes guiding our range to sink the freighters; we had nine 8-inch guns and could shoot up to 30 miles. One plane returned with 20 bullet holes and with the pilot shot in the foot."

The scout planes had pontoon bottoms and were ejected from the ship with a 60 foot catapult that used gun powder to shoot them down

Pontoon plane with USS Louisville *crew mates*

USS Louisville *in Aleutians, bound for Attu, May 1943*

Taken from USS Louisville *while preparing to bomb Kiska, August 1943*

a stationary sled protruding from the ship. When the planes returned, they landed in the water and went directly into a trailing cargo net. A crane then hooked onto the plane's eye attachment and brought it back on board. All of this took place while the ship was moving.

The *Louisville,* in pursuit, continued searching for and attacking the Japanese. "We bombarded the islands for the ground troop invasion," Earl said. "This was all in Alaska. We were up there freezing to death. Then we were on the equator sweating to death. Then they order us back [to Alaska] for another six-month tour. We would have to stop in at Pearl for warmer clothes in between [and] we missed the battle of Midway due to being there. We were [in Alaska] when we had only two hours of daylight; then we were there when we had two hours of darkness."

The *Louisville* returned to the Aleutians for sea bombardments at the battle of Attu Island in May, and at Kiska Island in August 1943. The Battle of Attu was the only land battle in WWII, fought on incorporated territory of the U.S. After two weeks fighting in Artic conditions, the Americans captured the island. Due to heavy casualties suffered at Attu, planners were expecting another costly operation at Kiska, but the Japanese realized the island was no longer defensible and had already evacuated. The Americans were not aware once they began their invasion and sea bombardments.

"We were later told we covered 180,000 miles in 18 months during that time. You got a thousand islands out there and we knew the Japanese were still there; we had to go back each time doing hard speed runs to give cover for the marines. I couldn't tell you the names of all of those islands, each one had a code name we went to, not the names you know today. The Japanese were underground and they finally sneaked out, and we took full control."

In calmer times, with Japanese out of the area, the *Louisville* would port into Kiska Island. But the collective stress, constant heavy travel, confinement, and the war itself took their toll on sailors.

"We'd pull into Kiska after being out at sea for way too long," Earl said. "Sailors would cut loose by going into town to drink. They would get drunk and then be picked up and put into the back of our 6x [six-wheeled vehicle] Army trucks to be taken back to the ship. But the sailors went unpunished," he added, "because the Navy knew they had kept us out too long. I was a little different, and I always felt this way about Kiska and the other ports we went into—I liked to visit, but I knew I wasn't completely free. I was cautious of what I did, had to avoid any kind of trouble."

After the Pearl Harbor attack and with a full-scale war ongoing, families often had minimal contact with their sons and relatives who were fighting. But the people wanted to know how their loved ones were doing and how the war was going.

"We didn't know the status of the war," Earl recalled. "I wrote letters to Mom and Penny and mail was sent to the FPO (Fleet Post Office) from the ship. We had people whose job at the post office was to go through each letter. We received mail only once a month, and incoming and outgoing mail had parts blacked out in fear of information getting into the enemy hands or morale being affected."

The West Coast FPO was located in San Francisco, while the East Coast office was in New York. Incoming mail was known as "V-mail," short for "victory mail." In a patriotic practice during WWII, letters from families were written on V-mail letter sheets and sent as thumbnail-sized microfilmed copies. That opened more cargo space for war materials. Once the V-mail was received overseas, it was delivered to the military personnel and expanded to one-quarter the original written letter size.

There was much for Earl to write about in the letters he sent home. The *Louisville,* now in the South Pacific, was searching for the "Tokyo Express," the name Allied Forces gave to the Japanese Navy because it used fast warships, such as destroyers, to deliver personnel, supplies, and equipment to Japanese forces near New Guinea and Solomon Islands. This was done quickly at night to avoid interception during the day.

"We couldn't use any personal radios, electric devices, or any lighting during this time," Earl said. "We only had light reflectors on the wall. We couldn't let the Japanese detect us. Our white suits were also dyed blue during this time to avoid any possible detection of us being seen. Fighting was tactical, but we were still in several battles out there in the South Pacific. One battle, we lost four cruisers in one night."

The *St. Louis* saved the *Louisville* that night near the Tulagi Strait just north of Guadalcanal. "A Japanese cruiser was within city blocks away of us, and we were about to be sunk," Earl said. "We were dead, but the *St. Louis* came in between us and fired." Earl took a moment as he recalled the battle, and cried. "We were almost hit twice with a torpedo while out there. We got hit with a torpedo one night again, but it didn't explode, it was a dud. You could see it cutting through the water. It knocked me off my feet. Another time a torpedo was fired, but the ship turned sharply to just avoid being hit."

He continued: "Radar, first being used at the beginning of the war, made it easier and protected us some from being hit. The *Louisville* bombarded a lot with Japanese ships always in the area. We hit Guadalcanal three [or] four times and the marines had to take it twice after it was handed it over to the Army and they lost it."

The Japanese observation or scout planes could be heard overhead and were known to sailors as "Washing Machine Charlies," because their engine sounded like a washing machine with its poorly synchronized one-cylinder sound. Also, U.S. ships in the region had to worry about kamikaze planes. The pilots would try to crash into the ships once being shot and spiraling downwards to avoid being captured or in a preplanned direct suicide mission.

Earl remembered a few such attempts and seeing other ships being hit, but he was able to avoid any kamikaze attack while at sea. The *Louisville,* later in the war, in one year would be hit by a total of three planes off the coast of the Philippines and Okinawa, Japan. "When it came to those crazy pilots, we knew their purpose was to die, and that they were going to try to take some of us with them when they did," Earl said.

The *Louisville* was amongst the convoy that traveled closely at times with the USS *Juneau* in the Guadalcanal Campaign. On November 13, 1942, during the Navy Battle of Guadalcanal and with the *Louisville* in the region, the *Juneau* was torpedoed and sunk, with five Sullivan brothers from Iowa dying together. A few weeks later during the Battle of Tassafaronga, the USS *New Orleans* was part of the taskforce with her flagship and sister ship, the USS *Minneapolis;* Bill was part of the crew.

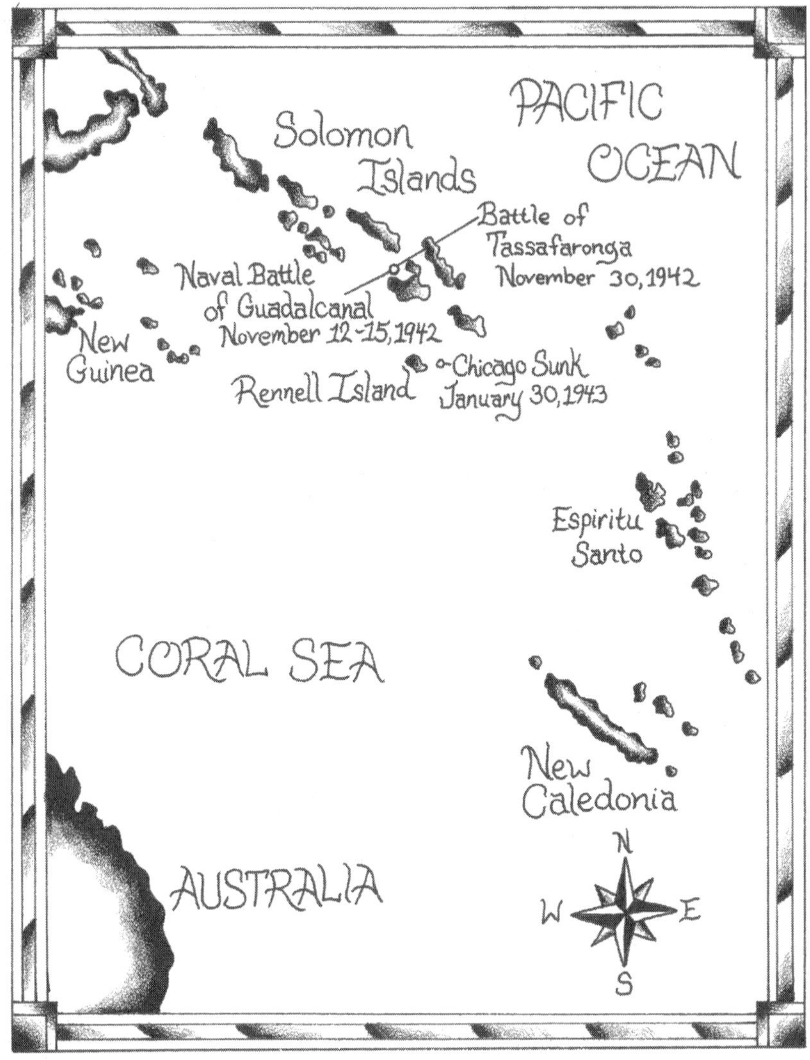

The *New Orleans* also lost its bow to a torpedo, killing three sets of three brothers. Soon after, the Navy banned brothers from serving together as shipmates. The U.S. military later instituted its sole survivor policy to prevent such incidents in the future.

The *Louisville* was commanded by Captain Charles Turner Joy, who later became an Admiral. The crew admired Joy, Earl said, because he would call them on deck before each mission and explain where they were going, and tell them everyone was coming back. They trusted Joy to get them out of hairy spots and make the difficult and best decisions.

"Joy was the only one that ever told us anything," Earl said. "He told us what our orders were, like finding that Tokyo Express, and what we needed to do. A story I will always remember about him is when we are out in the South Pacific and we shot down a Japanese plane with the pilot surviving and floating out in the water. Captain Joy was going to rescue and save the pilot, but the pilot pulled out a pistol and Joy instantly ordered the smaller millimeter guns to be turned on him.

"Captain Joy was a confident man as well. He'd never use a tug when coming into port; he would have the helmsman put the ship right up next to the dock like it was a motor boat."

On the night of Jan. 29, 1943, the *Louisville* and the USS *Chicago* were attacked by Japanese planes and separated from their fleet between Rennell and Guadalcanal Island. The *Chicago* was damaged, and the *Louisville,* using a steel hawser or cable, had been towing it to safety.

The *Louisville,* the *Chicago*'s sister ship, had taken a dud torpedo earlier near the Tulagi Strait, but still had the strength to transport. Both ships had been at Mare Island Naval Base months earlier for emergency gun replacement and repairs, but the *Louisville* was quickly ordered to Alaska without replacement guns because of the Japanese strong-hold in the Aleutians. Instead, the *Chicago* received the new guns, while the *Louisville* was sent with a civilian engineer to study the problem of the breach sticking on some guns. The civilian rode the ship for one month and many sailors were jealous because he was earning 33 dollars a day, more than they were.

Captain Charles Turner Joy

Earl recalled towing the *Chicago* all night. "She didn't have any engines. They could guide it, but there was no power," he said.

Japanese torpedo plane taking off for attack on the USS Louisville

"We were en route to nearby San Cristobal Island and had it in sight, then we got attacked again. Another five or six hours we could have had it there, but we got attacked by about 100 planes. We had two destroyers with us that were circling keeping submarines off us. We were one of the first ships to tow a ship the same size as ours, and we were doing it, but the captain told us to drop the tow and join the task-force. Vice Admiral Halsey ordered dropping of the tow."

During the tow, the *Louisville* and *Chicago* were running at five knots, a slow retreat to Espiritu Santo. Once the *Louisville* dropped the tow at

USS Chicago *being towed by USS* Louisville *after the Battle of Renell Island.*

8 a.m., it was picked up by the tug *Navajo* and briefly had the protection of six destroyers. In the early afternoon, after being hit by four Japanese torpedoes, the *Chicago* was forced to abandon ship. A little more than 1,000 men headed into the deep water below. The *Chicago* sunk stern first in just 20 minutes and 30 miles east of Rennell Island. Sixty-two of her crew died in these attacks. The Japanese had sent a final attack force of torpedo bombers, but could not find the other remaining ships that had been with the *Chicago*.

"The captain actually still wanted to save it by trying to beach it close to San Cristobal Island. It wasn't fifteen minutes after we dropped the tow. Planes began flying overhead to sink her. I don't know why, but the Japanese were dead set on sinking the *Chicago,* and they did."

The *Louisville* was able to port at Espiritu Santo without further incident. "Espiritu Santo was our major base out there and we didn't have too many problems because the Japanese weren't too thick in that location," Earl said. These attacks became known as the Battle of Rennell Island, and were one of the last major Naval battles between the Americans and Japanese.

The *Louisville,* on the offensive as the war progressed, moved closer to Japan and its occupied territories. One main territory, Iwo Jima, was an eight square mile island with three airfields, located 750 miles south of Tokyo. "We bombarded Iwo Jima with our 8-inch guns," Earl recalled. "The Japanese were very strong there. We were trying to lessen the resistance, so our marines could eventually invade. We could shoot up to 30 miles, but we were shooting from 20 miles onto the coast of Iwo Jima. This wasn't uncommon to bombard from that distance; we had sea battles with enemy ships from 25 miles apart, but also we fought some just next door." Towards the final stages of the war, the U.S. marines invaded, and after a fierce month-long fight, gained control of the island.

While serving on the *Louisville,* the death of his fellow shipmates hit Earl hard. He buried two sailors at sea, making the wooden platform for the first sailor and a scrap iron weight for the second, which is how the deceased were sunk into the ocean.

The first death came from an accident with one of the ship's five-inch guns. Earl recalled the ship coming to complete stop and flags lowered to half-mast. The deceased sailor received a small religious ceremony and a military ceremonial act of a unison volley from a firing party (the size of the party usually ranged from three to seven as determined by rank). The sailor received a seven member party along with a bugler who played "Taps," a musical piece used by the U.S. military to signify "lights out." The sailor was sewed up in a canvas bag with a 50-pound weight attached, and placed on a stationary wooden platform. Draped in an American flag, he was then tilted off into the sea.

"Everybody was crying," Earl said, "including the officers. It was misting rain. Crazy things were going through my head when you know you are putting somebody on the ocean floor for eternity."

The second burial came after an accident during a hazing incident. As Earl had done before, crossing the equator for the first time, sailors were "initiated," sometimes wearing a manila or frayed hemp rope as a hula skirt. The sailor's skirt caught fire and he was severely burned. He died a week later.

"How it caught on fire, I still don't know," Earl said. "I heard it was from somebody joking and chasing him with a match, and then I heard it was from the wind blowing lit ashes from a cigarette. It was not as bad as the first time, but still very heartbreaking."

Earl recalled being told of another ship that buried 33 sailors at sea. "That would be too much. I always hold respect for those deceased. If ever asked or given the honor to be a pallbearer for a person's final resting place, you never turn that down."

The USS *Louisville* was awarded 13 Battle Stars for service during WWII. After her decommission in 1946, Earl recalled, the ship was to be given to the city of Louisville, but it was too large to sail down the Ohio River. It was sold and scrapped in 1959.

CHAPTER SIXTEEN

THE RADIO MAN

Bill, Carl, and Earl were each defending their country, but Carl was the one completely separated from the family and seeing pretty hard times as well. While Earl and Bill patrolled and fought with the Navy in the Pacific, Carl was now in the Army. He had been in the Navy from 1936-1940 and then left the service. But the military kept you on notice during wartime, and Carl was given military conscription, an automatic one-year continuation, after Pearl Harbor (Carl was home in Louisville when the attack occurred) and was drafted into the Army. Carl wanted to return to the Navy, but an Army officer wouldn't release him. He went into the Army against his will, but they said he would be able to go to Ft. Knox and teach communications. The Army ended up not following through with what they said.

In the Army, Carl trained in the Republic of Ireland and later spent much of his time in Sicily, Northern Italy, and North Africa. Carl, of course, had always been the money man, but this time he would really have to earn it. Coming out of boot camp, Carl earned standard military pay, but just an additional 10 dollars a month for combat that became intense.

Carl was sent to North Africa out of boot camp, where he would spend a year, taking part in the invasion and then liberation. In the "North African" campaign—basically fighting the German Army in the North African desert; the Germans were led by General Field Marshall Erwin Rommel, who was known as the Desert Fox because of his successes. The battles were harsh; the German Army was seen as extremely tough by the Americans, and very advanced and sophisticated.

After success in North Africa, the American Army crossed the Mediterranean Sea, invading Italy and then traveling up the boot. Carl would be part of the fight at the Battle of Monte Cassino, also known as the Battle of Rome, a costly series of four battles from January 17 to May 18, 1943; the intention was to seize Rome. Carl fought there for a few months, and the Allies eventually were successful, but at a high price—55,000 men lost their lives during the Monte Cassino campaign.

Storming beachhead.

Carl then continued with his orders northwest, to fight at the Battle of Anzio, on the western coast of Italy, which began Jan. 22, 1944. The American Army completed their amphibious landing surrounded by mountains that were much more suitable for the German defense. They had expected a stay of only three days, but ended up not moving from their beach front position for four months. Conditions were bad for the Americans; they had to sleep in foxholes and those on the front line couldn't shower or change clothes for weeks—they were only able to change socks. "Carl told me he was supposed to know if the invasion was a success or failure within 72 hours. He didn't move three feet in three months. The Germans didn't push our guys back to sea, but we still just sat there," Earl said.

Injured soldiers.

While at the battle, Carl had conversations with the famous war correspondent Ernie Pyle, a Pulitzer Prize winner, who was later awarded the Purple Heart after being killed by a Japanese sniper. Today, his work is still recognized and his name is honored with a library and two historical sites. The School of Journalism at Indiana University, which he attended, is also named in his honor.

1942 - Earl's cousin Albert Henry Smith, in uniform, who was killed at Anzio.

Eventually on June 5, 1944, the American and Allied forces were successful in breaking through enemy lines. The Allied forces suffered 4,500 soldiers killed in action, 18,000 were wounded, with 6,800 prisoners taken or missing in action. The Smith brothers lost a first cousin, Albert Henry Smith, at this battle. Albert, the same age as Earl, was the son of "Uncle Ode," Jim W.'s brother Otis. Another Smith first cousin fought for the Army in Europe, and survived, but after taking the full impact from a bomb explosion, returned home severely burned and disfigured.

Carl was a tank radio man; he had two tanks blown out from under him the same day the Americans pushed into Italy, forcing him to return to the American line on foot after the second explosion. Carl and another tank crew member would carry another member of his five man crew, who was badly injured, through enemy lines at nighttime, finally reaching the American line days later. Sadly, the soldier would die of his wounds. Carl and his fellow crew member were awarded the Silver Star for the bravery he demonstrated in the attempt to save a fellow soldier. This award is the third-highest combat military decoration that can be awarded to a member of any branch of the United States Armed forces for valor in face of the enemy.

Many times, Carl had to carry around heavy radio equipment, manually hand-jamming radio frequencies in an attempt to confuse the Germans and Italians and clear a channel for the Americans. Often, to prevent enemy interception, he used a teletypewriter to send messages to the allied force commanders.

If the radio communications didn't work out in the field, he would have to string field wire from one tank to another to relay messages, and coordinates. Hanging wire from tank to tank was dangerous, because he was always exposed to enemy fire.

While in Guiliano, Italy, during 20 hours of continuous combat, Carl, under constant heavy enemy fire, dismounted his tank six times in a five hour period. On foot, and sometimes crawling, he would cover over 600 yards, checking radios and restoring lost communication among his outfit. Carl was also awarded the Bronze Star, the fourth-highest decoration awarded, for his actions of courage during this battle. Carl stayed in the village of Guiliano as the war in Europe ended, when Italian Prime Minister Benito Mussolini was executed in the town square.

"Carl had it much rougher than Bill and I," Earl admited. "He was on the front lines exposed to enemy fire. We could take showers, sleep in a bed, and eat three meals a day. Carl couldn't do that."

Carl and Earl never talked much about their experiences after the war. Once, Carl spoke about a job he was always excited to complete. He served as part of the third armored division, under the famous General, George S. Patton, and in North Africa and Italy, Carl transported General Patton several times in an Army Jeep. He once also talked about a much sadder story. Advancing quickly, with his outfit, he walked down a road in Africa next to a fellow soldier. As they advanced, they saw a dead soldier lying near the road. The soldier next to Carl had become instantly upset and said, "That was my brother." But they couldn't stop. They had to keep moving, following orders.

"You may not believe it, but what Carl had told me," Earl said, "those things did happen. I spoke to a fellow sailor once, who told me, just out of chance, he spotted his twin brother from a distance, standing out on another ship, and then, at that very second, watching him blown up by a torpedo."

More than one American G.I. who fought in Europe will account for these instances. The many dead, whether the enemy or American, from a distance were said to have resembled tree logs, and up close, sometimes soldiers were seen wearing wedding rings, along with pictures of their families poking out from their uniform shirt pockets. These images made many soldiers quickly realize each dead person was someone's husband, father, son, or brother.

Since Carl worked in communications, he wasn't restricted to land. He spent time in the air as well, and logged many hours flying with a pilot. Once, he allowed a fellow radio man to take a flight in his place to help him accumulate his required hours. The plane took off for Guam from Hawaii, but crashed, killing the two men.

When the war ended, Carl was on the French border. The Army had a points system and he had enough to come home, but he was declared

Staff Sergeant Carl Smith, Italy, March, 1945

"essential" and had to stay in Europe as part of the occupying forces. Carl eventually left the Army in 1945 as a staff sergeant.

Before entering the Navy, Carl wanted to go to an agriculture college and become a farmer. Carl joined the Navy, so he could save money. Once discharged and home from the Navy, Carl married a girl from Caneyville, Ora Maye Embry, just before he joined the war effort. Ora Maye's father was a minister and member of the state legislature. She was younger than Carl and in Earl's class (she admitted having a school girl crush on Carl's younger brother at first). Once Carl returned home, they would begin a family, raising their two children, Kevin and Shannon.

After returning from the war, Carl studied at a local business college on the G.I. Bill and started a few businesses' along the way. He owned a restaurant, The Corner Lunch Room, in Louisville, where he was able to employ some of his nieces and nephews while they were in high school and college. Carl eventually became successful in banking. Carl and Ora Maye would be together until their deaths.

Ora Maye, 1938

Chapter Seventeen

USS *BLISS*

USS Bliss

Earl became a commissioned Chief Warrant Officer in 1943 and was transferred off the *Louisville* to a General G.O. Squire-Class transport, the USS *Bliss* AP-131. The *Bliss* was a newly constructed ship, and Earl went on the shakedown cruise. She went on to receive a Battle Star for her WWII service. On the *Bliss*, Earl was head of the repair division, working as an assistant to the First Lieutenant in the engineering department.

He estimated that he traveled 288,000 miles in 18 months on the *Bliss*, making 11 round-trip trans-Atlantic voyages, and transporting around 3,500 sailors and marines. Earl and the *Bliss* shared many adventures along the way. In the North Atlantic, he saw large icebergs, as well as humpback whales, and bottleneck dolphins swimming next to the ship, on a regular basis. Sometimes the ship saw 50-foot ground-swells in stormy waters. The *Bliss*, painted grey, black, and white for camouflage, spent much of its time avoiding German submarines in the Atlantic, particularly off the coasts of England and France. Once, while crossing the English Channel, the *Bliss*'s escort dropped 22 depth charges (anti-submarine explosive device). In 1944, the *Bliss* forced a German submarine to the surface near Gibraltar and escorted it, guns drawn, on a week-long trip into Boston.

Earl was at sea when he learned of the death of President Roosevelt in 1945. Grieving, he was concerned by the horrible timing, because the country was still involved in a war. The *Bliss* continued on with her orders.

The *Bliss* was involved in transporting troops to Naples, Italy, and then docked for a few days. Earl saw Army troops camped out in an open field and tents close to the port. They were playing poker and he began to walk towards them. He then heard a guy say, "That's Smitty's brother," referring to Carl. They told Earl that Carl had left for the front lines just the day before, and they offered to take him there in a jeep, but Earl worried he would miss the *Bliss*. Sailors never knew how long they would stay in port; when a captain received orders, the ship promptly departed to its next destination. Earl also frankly admitted he was concerned about being on the Army front lines. He and Carl did not see each other again until 1946.

Earl had a terrifying adventure when the *Bliss* got lost in the Bermuda Triangle, a triangular region in the western north Atlantic Ocean known for mysterious disappearances of planes and navy vessels. Earl had gone through the infamous area many times and it was always rough. On one occasion, however, a seven-day run from Gibraltar to New York before Christmas, the ship got lost.

"The navigator could not get a fix on us," Earl said. "He didn't know where we were. There weren't no stars, no moon, no nothing. Just nothing out there. The Captain, Burton Davis, said, 'Thirty-three years in the Navy, and this is the worst I ever been in.' We finally broke radio silence to Washington D.C. and a Navy plane was sent to find us. We were shooting out radio beams trying to be found.

"That's how we found our way. A seven-day run took us 15 days to make. We were in a typhoon, in the eye of the storm, and couldn't get out. The water spray went down our smokestack and put the fire out in our boiler room. The worst part was that the ship cracked and took on 55,000 gallons of sea water. The ship took water in the bow and the stern was flooded to counteract. We lost 16 miles back toward Africa, according to the navigator. We were trying to run at 16 knots against the wind. A ship at full speed would usually run at 32 knots, and in normal conditions travelled at 20 knots. We usually ran at that speed."

After getting tossed sideways and nearly upside down throughout the storm, the ship went to Staten Island for repairs. Earl was part of the crew charged with repairing it. Once docked, members of the crew were allowed to call their families.

"We had horrible weather on the *Bliss*," Earl recalled. "I don't know how we stood it. I saw the expansion joint that kept the ship from breaking in half move over an inch on the main deck. It was scary." And storms weren't the only thing they had to worry about. "Our problem was we ran alone a lot, with no escort. We never knew if we were in hostile waters or not."

Because of the war's heavy fighting demands, many reserves were called in. Some reserves had recently graduated from college and officer training school or were civilian working-professionals just out of college. Earl's boss, a lawyer from Pottstown, Pennsylvania, was a full lieutenant he called Raker.

"We brought in these reserves who were college kids," Earl said. "A lot of these college boys who came in didn't know their left foot from their right. I liked Raker, but I didn't know how smart he was. I soon realized I knew things he didn't know about sea life and also being at war. It sometimes took more than just education to be a sailor. I didn't know why upper command would put him and others like that in those positions during war time."

There was a death on the *Bliss* while Earl served. A lieutenant died of natural causes and was kept in the lower deck freezer until the ship docked in New York after traveling from the Pacific. Earl recalled the man having hallucinations and becoming aggressive. He was separated from the rest of the men, and Earl remembered warning the doctor, a husky man from Michigan, who examined the man, that he was dangerous. Earl didn't know how he died, but heard it may have been from an infection that spread to his brain. Capt. Davis was determined to return him to his family for a proper burial.

Captain Burton Davis, circa 1943

Earl described Davis as a tall, slender man with skinny legs: he loved to drink. Docked in Africa, Earl once saw Davis return from a night of heavy drinking, crawling on his hands and knees up the gangway and refusing help from the marines. The scene repeated itself on more than one occasion. After such nights, he went straight to his room and did not return until the next day. At dock, Earl was often the Officer on Deck when Davis left the ship and Earl also was put on sea watch, responsible for keeping the ship on course.

On one of those occasions, a sudden wind storm came up and quickly dissipated. Ropes tied to the dock tore, and the bow began drifting from the dock, which broke the gangway in half and blew it into the water. Earl was prepared to drop anchor to prevent the ship from drifting further, because the engines were off and it would take time to start them up and return to the dock. When Davis drove up in a Jeep with two civilians, Earl thought he would get chewed out. But Davis was sober, and after hearing what happened, and with the civilians saying storms did come up from time to time, Davis just patted him on the back. Earl never knew if they were telling the truth about the storms or were simply trying to help a sailor, but he was grateful to stay out of trouble. "Even though Davis drank a lot," Earl said, "he was still an all-round sailor and a captain with integrity."

Some of the bearded crew of the USS Bliss, *circa 1943*

The *Bliss* had a notable crew at the time, including the son of U.S. Postmaster General Frank C. Walker; William "Billy" Sullivan, future owner of the NFL's New England Patriots Football team; and Phillip Willkie, the son of 1940 presidential candidate Wendell Willkie.

Earl recalled being at sea when a destroyer picked up Phillip Willkie to transport him to New York after his father's death. Wendell Willkie had suffered several heart attacks while traveling by train from his native Indiana to New York City. Earl also remembered conversations with French Actor Jean-Pierre Aumont, who was serving in the French Army. In the United States, Aumont was best known as the star of the American film *Song of Scheherazade.* Earl also served with Commodore P.V.H. Weems, who is credited with inventing many navigational instruments.

Earl recalled a former University of Pennsylvania football player who taught him to use the Sexton navigational tool, and a "hillbilly" from West Virginia who inherited one million dollars from a family business that sold fire equipment. Many more Earl could not name, though their faces and actions were etched in his memory for the rest of his life.

He remembered a young orphaned Italian boy wearing a tailor-made uniform and who served as a U.S. Army battalion mascot. Someone had snuck him aboard in a duffle bag, and he was not discovered until they reached American soil. Earl later learned he was adopted by an American Army officer and grew up in Texas.

He also recalled a similar scenario with animals being hidden on board. Mongoose, for example, were brought on to kill non-indigenous snakes and rats when they returned to Hawaii, but the captain found out and ordered them thrown overboard.

Many German, Italian, and American prisoners of war were transported to the United States through the harbor at New York. The German and Italian prisoners were taken to POW camps around the country.

"The officers were kept in the state room" Earl said, "and enlisted men were kept in the hole of the ship. I would see the officers run freely while on the ship, and the German officers were always very well dressed and spoke good English. I would talk to them a lot. One officer told me, 'I have probably been to New York City even more than you, but I got caught on the wrong side.'"

CHAPTER EIGHTEEN

A SAILOR'S LIFE

Earl saw his Navy ships as small-scale working cities, with 1,000 to 2,000 male military personnel on board. "A Navy ship is like a big factory; everybody works," Earl said. "When Bill and I were on the *Argonne*, even though it was before the war, it still felt like we worked all the time, and didn't get to socialize much with the rest of the ship. You only knew people in your division; we worked in the R division. R was for repair, and it was part of the engineering division. In the department we had all metal, all piping, and stuff like that. We were in charge of all the water; we repaired pipes, and even made lockers. I was considered a ship fitter, with pipefitting as one of my duties."

During wartime, and out to sea, everyone stayed busy with the war effort; a sailor sometimes worked around the clock and tried to sleep when not working. "During wartime, it's a little different," Earl said. "There are no certain hours, no bedtime or nothing. You're just seven days a week, 24 hours a day. But during peacetime, when the U.S. military was not involved in any war, you worked eight hours a day and then if you're lucky, you didn't stand the watch that night. Usually, every other night you got a four-hour watch. What you watched, I don't know. Sometimes you watched over the engine room or would be on security watch patrolling the ship. You're still on alert all the time even though it is peacetime."

Ships had many sailors, and privacy and space were often limited; enlisted sailors had only a storage locker and a bed. Sleeping quarters were typically open, with as many as 50 sailors sleeping in bunk beds, or in a "rack," sometimes stacked four bunks high. On the *Louisville,* Earl slept on the top bunk.

Ships continuously had some type of maintenance and cleaning being performed. Sailors were often ordered to swab the deck, even during stormy weather. At times, Earl thought his ships' decks were clean enough to eat off. They had doctors and sick bays, dentists, chaplains, a barber and laundry service. When a sailor needed personal items, he went to the "geedunk" stand, military slang for a quick food store, with items such as cigarettes, toiletries, ice cream, and candy.

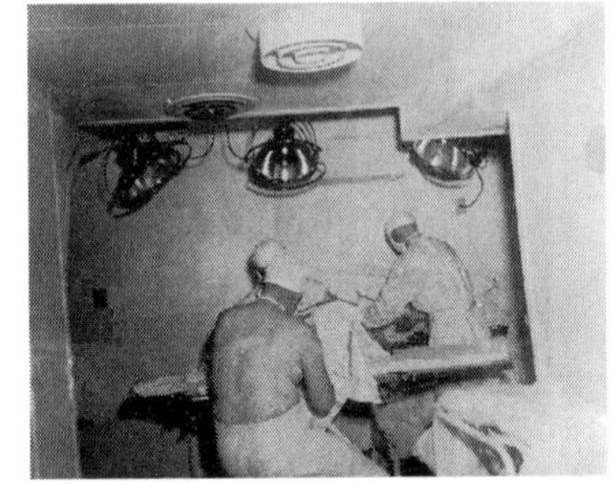

Operating room on ship

"A candy bar and a pack of cigarettes cost five cents," he said, "while a carton of cigarettes was ten cents." The ship also had a brig, or jail, for sailors found guilty of breaking military law.

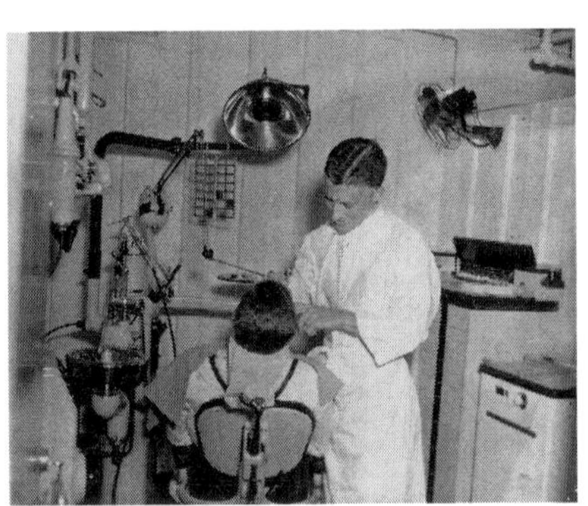

Dentist on ship

"Head," was the Navy term for bathroom, because in the early days they had been located in the ship's bow, or head. The head was a latrine or trough; water ran through it continuously before exiting a hole on the side of the ship. Like showers, the head was open and offered no privacy.

"Sometimes a guy would take too long sitting and doing his business," Earl said, laughing at the memory. "We'd put newspaper in the water at one end. It would flow down to the guy sitting and rub against his butt. He'd be startled and then would jump right up."

During war time on the *Bliss*, Earl remembered sailors eating while standing up in the mess hall, the cafeteria. A small tray table would slide down a metal pipe to sit food on. Wooden tables were in the mess hall, but sailors avoided them if the ship's radar made contact with a submarine.

"The Navy finally realized that wood splinters were worse than steel when a ship was hit," Earl said, recalling how efforts were made at the beginning of the war to get rid of as much wood as possible. There was also the issue of constant motion. Ships rocked back and forth, prompting trays in the mess hall to slide back and forth and making some sailors sick.

"Ships then didn't have stabilizers like you see on bigger ships today," Earl said. "You had to anchor your food tray with your fist." He mentioned a story that was unfortunate for those involved, but funny nonetheless. "We had bad weather one day, and I saw a marine becoming sick. Then his neighbor's food tray slid down in front of him just as he threw up." It was hard to avoid spilling things, including hot coffee. Earl saw many guys burned.

Sailors in the South Pacific often slept on deck because of the heat. The ships had large fans to circulate sea air, but the men still slept on deck because they could get sick from the excessive heat inside the ship.

Also, because of the high temperatures and heavy rainfall, the Pacific was a breeding ground for disease. With sailors living in close quarters and also transporting personnel who brought some diseases on board, many of the men contracted malaria, dysentery and tuberculosis. Intestinal parasites were also a problem. Records show that 15,000 soldiers contracted these parasites during the war, mostly those fighting in the Pacific, and usually after eating poorly cooked meat or fish.

Earl remembered a shipmate and friend visiting the *Bliss*'s sick bay after having stomach pains that were determined to be an intestinal tapeworm. He began to receive treatment and Earl would have no idea what he was about to see, although it had been documented in medical books before; the tapeworm a few days later, would find a way to exit while Earl and his friend were walking onshore.

"I don't tell many people this story, because it is a little sickening to talk about." Earl said, chuckling at the memory. "It crawled out the bottom of his pants leg. People can believe what they want, but I know what I saw."

Diseases weren't the only thing ships had to worry about. Sometimes sailors would fall overboard in rough weather, but the Navy was always prepared. "I remember one guy falling, and he was picked up by the ship trailing us; he didn't drown," Earl said. "A sailor eventually learns the sea and knows what to do and not to do on deck. If it was bad weather or shooting of the big guns, we didn't go out. If things were good at night, you were free to go anywhere on the ship if not on watch. Even though they began to all look the same, I still saw many beautiful night skies while I circled the globe."

Getting exercise at sea was important and encouraged, but it depended on which ship you were on. Earl's ships had only a punching bag, while others had more gym equipment. Sailors were allowed recreational swimming, but only in port, or out to sea if they had protection from sharks. In peace time, ships had teams—boxing, wrestling, football, basketball, rowing, and swimming that competed when ships were on shore. Basketball was often played on the ships as well.

Ships also competed in categories such as engineering and maritime warfare. This was all for the Battle "E," or the Battle Efficiency award, based on a year-long evaluation of battle readiness. The ship that excelled over the others would display a red "E" on its smokestack (for engineering) or a black "E" (for maritime warfare).

Sometimes the competition got physical. After the *Louisville* towed the *Chicago,* Earl and the rest of the crew got 10 days of R and R in Wellington, New Zealand. Earl assumed it was their reward for the tow, but never knew for sure. A group of marines had fallen back there for R and R as well. New Zealand had a gas shortage, and the Navy gave gas to the locals in exchange for housing sailors and showing them around. With three other sailors, Earl stayed for three days with the top horticulturist in New Zealand, who allowed them to use his car around town, although Earl had to figure out how to use the right side steering wheel and driving on the left side of the road.

The marines began to assert their presence by giving the sailors orders, moving in on the local women the sailors had met, and making fun of the Navy. In downtown Wellington, tempers grew. Earl and other sailors were involved in a street fight with a group of marines.

"We had about ten guys and they had about ten guys," he said. "During the middle of the fight, a marine was going to hit my friend with the brass buckle on his belt. I mounted him and took him down. An older lady walking down the sidewalk got in the middle of us and screamed for us to stop—and we did. She said her dad had fought in the Boer War; she didn't want to see us fighting." [The Boer Wars, were two short-lived wars, ending in 1902, between the British Empire and the descendants of Dutch settlers in South Africa.]

"I had fought the marines before and once was hit in the head with a big bottle of some kind of alcohol, out of nowhere," Earl said. "We would fight with them, but we knew they were our best outfit, definitely the toughest."

Needless to say, living for multiple months or more on a ship with several hundred people meant close quarters and required a lot of patience and camaraderie. On board, sailors passed the time by playing pinochle and acey-deucy, a form of backgammon. Earl played a lot of this game and nothing else. He recalled heavy gambling on the *Bliss*, though it was forbidden. Sailors held poker games in different rooms around the ship, and Earl recalled that the house always got a cut.

"Money didn't mean anything to many sailors, because you never knew if you were going to make it back home," Earl said.

On the *Bliss*, a little more than a year before the war ended, Earl was in the port of Cherbourg, France, and ran into a childhood friend. Junior Fentress was from Falls of Rough. He had joined the Army and now that he was in Europe, was scared about the war, particularly the unknown. "I consoled Junior, and then bet him 10 dollars that he'd be back home in a year. I didn't know the war would end, but I wanted to make him feel better that he was going to survive." Junior did make it home and Earl happened to run into him on Market Street in Louisville. Junior was good for it. "He pulled out the money," Earl said, laughing at the memory, "and paid me right on the street."

Enlisted sailors had to salute and say good morning when they approached an officer, and this continued throughout the day.

"When we would see an officer we would have to salute and address them accordingly with great respect," Earl said. "If he was a commander and his last name was Jones, we'd say, 'Commander,' or 'Commander Jones.' We would always answer, 'Yes, sir' or No, sir' if a question was asked."

The same held true when Earl became an officer on the *Bliss*, though one time the promotion nearly got him into trouble. Officers on the *Bliss* were allowed to wear pants with pockets. He couldn't do that before and he had a hard time getting used to it.

One day as he stood with his hands in his pockets, the ship's commander, a big Texan with 40 years in the Navy, approached and he wasn't pleased.

"You need to take your hands out of your pockets," he said, "or I am going to fill your pockets full of sand and tie your hands in there for 30 days." Earl got the message and learned to keep his hands where they could be seen.

Earl with hand in his pocket, on the Indian Ocean, 1945

Though an officer, at times Earl didn't act like one. He sometimes wanted to joke with those aboard. Once, while sailing into the New York Harbor, he told some newly enlisted and young wide-eyed sailors coming into the harbor for the first time, to watch the Statue of Liberty closely because she would sometimes drop her right arm. They followed orders, but Earl always felt bad about telling them that.

Bill, Raye, and Earl at Latin Quarters Night Club, New York City, 1945

Chapter Nineteen

THE WAR'S END

When the European phase of the war ended, May 8, 1945, better known as VE Day for victory in Europe, Earl was on the *Bliss* just off the coast of Cherbourg, France. Italian Prime Minister Benito Mussolini had been captured, and executed on April 28, 1945. That was followed by the death of German leader Adolf Hitler, who shot himself on April 30, 1945.

"Hitler was a monster and crazy. We had heard that he killed himself down in a bunker in Berlin," Earl remembered, but "we didn't know if it was a rumor or not. When we found out it was true, we were more excited that the war may eventually end, not really from the death of him."

On August 6 and August 9 of 1945, two atomic bombs were dropped on the Japanese cities of Hiroshima and Nagasaki to prevent an American land invasion into Japan to end the war. When it all finally ended, August 14, 1945, or VJ Day (victory over Japan), Earl was heading to the harbor in New York after being out in the Atlantic. He always remembered the confetti still flying in the air when they arrived a day later.

"We were very glad the danger of the war was over, but not just overly excited," Earl said. "We knew we weren't going home that soon. Europe had been destroyed and now Japan had felt the major effects of the war."

For the world, World War II was the deadliest military conflict in history. After the war ended, exact numbers were hard to fully determine, but it is estimated that the total death toll ranged from 62 to 78 million.

In Europe, it was very deadly, with over half the death toll coming from there. The death toll for the American military was around 420 thousand, and for militaries worldwide, it was 22 to 25 million.

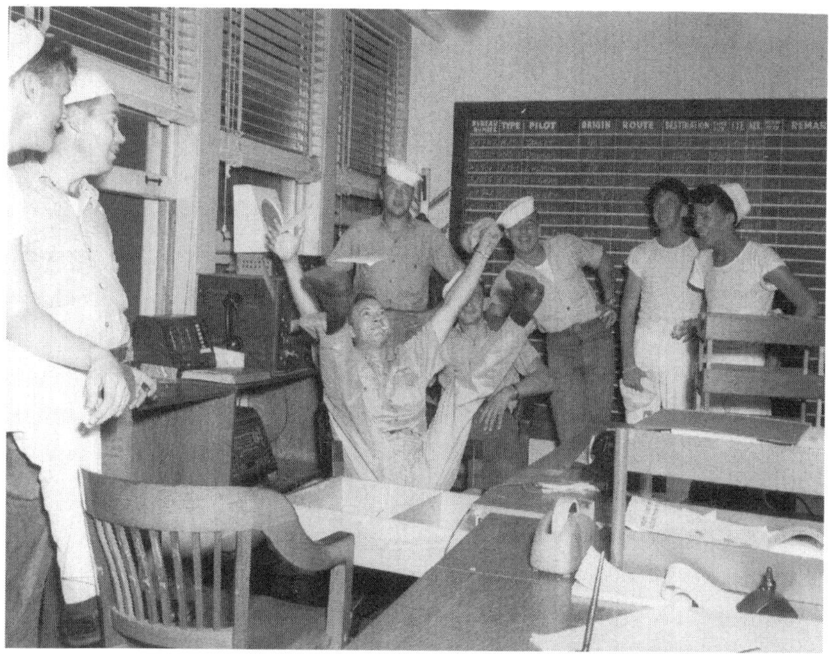

Sailors celebrating Japan's surrender and the war's end, 1945

Chapter Twenty

BACK TO THE NAVY

The war was over. After serving on the USS *Bliss*, Earl considered taking his discharge in 1946, but 89 days later, after seeing the poor job market availability for civilians, he reenlisted. The military gave him 100 dollars a month for three months, which was to end at the 90 day mark. There were many G.I.s out looking for work after the war, which made it difficult. Reenlisting, since he was a warrant officer, cost Earl four ranks, but the hiatus was not considered a break in service.

Earl's attempt at civilian life was after Bill did the same thing. He, too, was out 89 days and reenlisted, dropping in rank to E-7, Chief Petty Officer. Had he not stayed out for that time period, Earl believed, Bill would have been on direct course to make Lieutenant.

Though Earl had left high school early to join the Navy, he was later told that his military experience was equal to a high school diploma.

"When I applied for civilian jobs when I got out, they'd ask if I had a high school education," he said. "I would say yes, because the Navy told me if you have made officer you have a high school diploma. They even told me I had what was equal to two years of college, but there were never any documented papers go with it.

"I have to be honest; it felt strange trying to be a civilian after being away from home and off fighting in the war for so long. Even when I finally saw my family, they seemed different, like they had all changed.

They sounded so funny to me. Then, I realized I was the one that had changed," Earl said.

Upon returning in 1946, Earl joined the crew of the *ARD 10*, an engineless auxiliary repair dock vessel that was pulled by a tug ship. These floating dry docks would provide a dry docking area to repair damaged vessels while keeping the crew stationary.

After Earl boarded in San Francisco, the ship was tugged for 30 days to Panama where Earl and the rest of the crew were stationed. He had been through the Suez Canal many times; now, he was stationed near the Panama Canal and could watch its daily operations.

"I remember seeing the big Navy carriers squeeze through the locks with only an inch on each side for clearance. During that time, the Panama Canal determined the size of ships built in America." Although the United States built and owned the canal, U.S. ships had to pay to go through it. "I didn't understand that," Earl said.

Penny and Earl already had a daughter, Montee Marie, who was born in 1943, in Los Angeles. Child number two, arrived in 1946, while they were living in Panama. They named him James Earl Smith, Jr. (later known as Jimbo), and he was born at Coco Solo Hospital, a Navy submarine base on the northwest side of the Panama Canal; Earl paid for Penny to join him while he was stationed there.

"What was good about the military was that when my kids were born in a military hospital, everything was covered except the food eaten. Sometimes even that was covered," Earl said. "My children who were born on base, each cost me less than 20 dollars at the most. My son Jim didn't cost me anything."

After the war he'd wanted to become a family man, and before he went to Panama, he purchased a home in Los Angeles, four blocks away from the LAX airport. But the airport expanded and forced Earl to buy a second home near Inglewood, and six blocks in another direction from the airport.

The house overlooked Culver City, in the valley of West Los Angeles. Culver City was known primarily for its movie studios such as MGM (later Sony). Earl could also see the Howard Hughes Aircraft Co., but he ended up not living there, and he rented it out while he was away, with Penny staying with her mother or with him. Earl, in attempt to settle in a little more, joined the freemasonry of Los Angeles during this time.

Earl was ordered to Charleston, SC, Naval Yard, when Jim Jr. was only two months old. Earl and his family flew from Panama to Pentucket River, MD, and then on to Louisville to visit. They took a Greyhound bus into Charleston to begin their lives together as a family.

For this assignment, Earl was in charge of maintenance of the Bachelor Officers Quarters. Those without families on base lived there, including many high-ranking officers. Earl spent time a lot of time with them, playing ping pong, though he wasn't supposed to associate with those of a high rank.

Penny was ready to get back to Southern California, and Earl soon received a transfer to Monterey, in Northern California. He was ordered to a refresher course in Line School, which was held for high-ranking officers at the Del Monte Hotel, an elaborate Navy owned hotel in Monterey.

During his time there, he utilized the assistance of planes overhead to earn extra money from net fishing. A pilot would spot schools of fish and give him the location and type of fish. Earl and a group of fisherman would go and drop the nets. He also earned money washing dishes and unloading and loading freighters. Other G.I.s made fun of him for taking these jobs for money, but he'd simply say, "When I write a check, I don't worry about it bouncing."

After line school, Earl became an instructor in the cargo department at the U.S. Naval Prison at Mare Island Naval base in Vallejo, CA. He was in charge of teaching prisoners how to handle cargo, with the goal of teaching them a trade before their return back into the military or to civilian life.

CHAPTER TWENTY-ONE

USS *BUCK*

USS Buck

Earl completed his teaching assignment and was ordered to the USS *Buck* DD-761, an Allen M. Sumner Class destroyer. Though it was peace time, Earl had many memorable experiences while on the USS *Buck*. Along with the destroyer *John W. Thomason* DD-760, the *Buck*, run by

Captain Ellsworth N. Smith, escorted the carrier USS *Boxer* to the Far East. The *Boxer* was the carrier of the Navy's first jet operations at sea.

The *Boxer* continued jet operations and the *Buck* would pick up pilots who missed the carrier during the escort trip to the Far East. While escorting, the *Buck* was hit by an oil tanker, which tore a gun hub loose. While off to Japan for repairs, the ship tore off a propeller—or in Navy terms, a "screw,"—while backing in to dock at Yokosuka Naval base in Yokosuka, Japan.

The *Buck* had two large bronze propellers, which mobilized the ship (larger ships had four). So the crew had to prepare the gun hub and also wait for a new propeller; the *Buck* remained docked in Japan for two weeks while a part was flown from the United States, and another week for repair. Earl recalled the Japanese had a frightening way of repairing the ship; they used high bamboo scaffolding only tied with bark. But they completed the work safely, first the gun tub and then the propeller.

Earl vividly recalled the *Buck*'s Captain at the time; he was unlike any other officers he had served under. It was required, and they understood, that sailors must give loyalty and obedience to the ship's captain, who had full authority on his ship in all circumstances.

"Captain Smith was the captain of the ship when we tore up our propeller," Earl said. "He was a little crazy, I thought. Smith was a different kind of captain. Destroyers rode rough and sometimes sailors would get sick just returning from leave, but I remember him, even though a captain, staying seasick all the time. He'd take all the pills out of the sick bay."

Earl and the crew never knew where Smith came from. They felt he captained and drove the ship like it was a car. Earl always thought he must have come from a freighter.

"One time, we got orders to return to Pearl from Guam and he told us we were pulling out at 2 p.m. and we better be on it," Earl said. "At 2 p.m. he tooted that whistle four times and we pulled out. We left Guam at full speed with us hardly able to even stand up. We hit Pearl, then he decided to head down to San Diego. The total trip from Guam, and into Pearl, then San Diego was a five-day trip; it took us three."

Earl remembered his visits to Japan after the war and how the Japanese military were initially friendly and would bow to the Americans when they stepped onto Japanese soil. However, after a short time the mood changed and they became rude to American sailors. Earl remembered more than once a member of the Japanese military making an obscene gesture toward him. He never understood why they even bowed initially, because he knew they resented the Americans.

He visited Tokyo and saw the Tokyo Imperial Palace, the primary residence of the Emperor of Japan. He remembered it as similar to the Vatican, a city within a city, and that it was a majestic place with a wooden draw bridge and a moat.

While docked, Earl spent time with the locals, too. "The Japanese civilians were nice people," he remembered. "I went into some of their homes. They didn't have furniture, and we had to sit on the floor. We had to take off our shoes, also. I remember they rode a lot of bicycles to get everywhere. The military was trained to fight to the death during the war for the Emperor and the land of the Rising Sun, but these civilians were very cordial to us."

The Imperial Palace in Tokyo, 1947

The Great Buddah of Kamakura in Tokyo, 1947

Many of the *Buck*'s crew associated closely with Japanese locals, but sometimes it was just for their financial gain. Cigarettes, 50 cents a carton on board, were valuable on the Japanese black market. Japanese citizens were on the ship often, buying cartons of cigarettes from the sailors and smuggling them away under overalls and loose clothing. Captain Smith participated as well, and was seen taking a load to his Jeep every day, which he'd take ashore and sell to the Japanese.

"I watched Smith and the other sailors bring the Japanese locals on board to sell those cigarettes and you would see them leaving with cartons stuffed everywhere," Earl said. "Under their shirt and coat, in their pockets, and in their pants; they put them just everywhere. It was quite obvious. I was no angel, but I never smoked. My mom broke me of that long ago. Mostly I was just too scared to try and do that."

Japanese toilet in Tokyo. Photo from Earl's visit after the war, 1947

The *Buck* was off the coast of the Korean peninsula, after docking in the Incheon Harbor near

Seoul, South Korea, and on her return to the United States, she got caught in a massive typhoon. This was at the end of the trip for propeller repairs.

The storm began tearing away parts of the wooden deck. Below deck at the bow, a single-line bucket brigade formed to empty the water that was quickly coming aboard. The *Buck* received scheduled dry dock maintenance to take care of minor damage, and for general upkeep and protecting the ship, but this storm was very strong, and the *Buck* eventually landed at Guam for emergency repairs.

The *Buck* made two trips to Korea within a few months. It was quickly called back after two ships were damaged in a collision and were unable to patrol the waters. Earl recalled being out in San Diego on Sunday, then hearing the orders that they were to leave port for Korea at 7:30 Monday morning. Sailors never could go too far away from port, because of these sudden orders. After Earl left the *Buck*, the *Buck* had a collision itself, colliding with the *Thomason* while traveling at 22 knots, causing multiple injuries to the crew and excessive damage to the ship.

"When you went into port, if you're important, you go to shore," Earl said. "If you are a regular sailor you stay aboard or maybe are allowed off—sometimes just one day, sometimes two days, and sometimes every other day. It's all depending on your commanding officer and supposed length of stay, but that can all change in an instant."

After serving on the *Buck*, Earl decided to leave the Navy. He was discharged at the Great Lakes Naval Base in North Chicago. As a sailor, he had risen in rank from apprentice seaman to Chief Warrant Officer, grade four by December 1944, and made Chief Warrant Officer in six years, all by the age of 23. This was a feat in a competitive situation, though he said the active war aided his advancement. Still, he was one of the youngest in the United Stated Navy to attain that status.

After discharge, Earl returned to southern California and tried working a regular job. He wanted to be a family man and a father, spending quality time with his children instead of being gone constantly. He was a truck driver for a produce man, making little money to support his family. This lasted only a few months before he re-enlisted back into the military.

Chapter Twenty-two

THE THINGS HE SAW

Earl's buddy in Jamaica, circa 1939

Many times Earl visited countries and was not restricted to a ship, so he went out to enjoy the sites and culture. While on the *Argonne*, and new to the Navy, he always enjoyed his early visits to Kingston, Jamaica, and the Caribbean, and hanging out with the locals. He would also stop in South America, Egypt, and other parts of Africa during his travels.

During his early Navy years, on multiple trips to Guantanamo Bay, Cuba, he enjoyed watching the Cuban fights, the sailors called "smokers." Earl had been a boxer for a short time as a teenager, representing Portland Park in Louisville. He would joke, after taking a good whipping from a boy representing Boone Square Park, he had since retired.

Earl did feel awkward when in downtown Cherbourg, France. He was given a privacy shield after asking if a bathroom was close by. It was standard for locals to use the open sewer system that ran through the city.

Cuban smokers, circa 1939

Earl remembered visiting India four or five times while in the Navy. Once while on the USS *Bliss* and off the coast of Mumbai, India, he got grounded on a sand bar, which required the crew to empty the ship's freshwater to eliminate weight.

Karachi, India, 1939

In Karachi, India, (now in Pakistan) he was amused by the many King Cobra snake charmers on the streets, and he also took his first rickshaw ride. It was pulled by a young boy, and Earl got upset when the other passenger kicked the boy to go faster.

Earl's rickshaw ride in Karachi, 1939

Earl also saw other things he didn't enjoy, such as the cremation of deceased bodies, which he had never seen before. People over five years old who died were placed in "Burning Ghats." It was custom for the bodies to be placed on individual pieces of wood, with the arms and legs protruding. Wood was used in exact amounts, to avoid wasting it. Bodies were

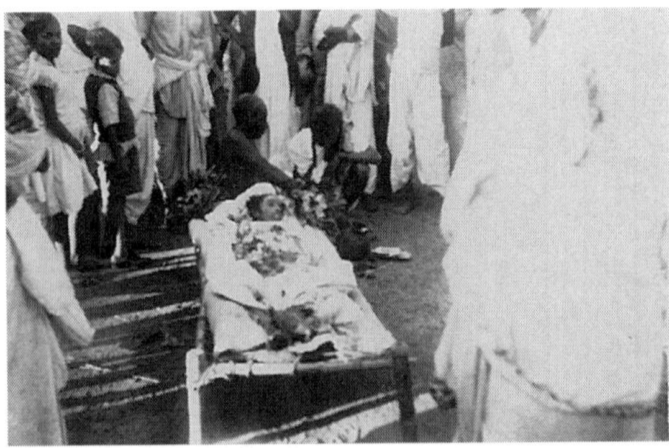

Burning ghat with girl, 1939

Burning ghat with girl's ashes, 1939

placed over small open pits, and the public could watch. The cremations were usually done near a body of water. Earl saw a cremation, of a beautiful young woman who looked to be between 18 to 21 years old. Ashes in this area were placed in the Lyari and Malir rivers; this was believed to bring purification to the deceased.

The bodies of children who died before the age of five were thrown into the two rivers as well, where people also bathed and washed clothes. Earl remembered seeing hungry vultures flying over and sometimes landing on these young bodies.

The war had taken its toll on many countries, and for years afterward Earl saw the post-war effects of unstable regions. The Japanese had treated the Hong Kong citizens horribly during their occupation, with the population reduced from 1.6 million to 600,000 at the time of the Japanese surrender. Many Hong Kong citizens were starved and/or executed.

Earl saw poverty and severe hunger in multiple countries, but in Hong Kong, a starving group of women offered to paint the ship's bow up to the waterline in exchange for a chance to scavenge through the sailor's food scraps after meal-time. They were allowed to do it, but Earl told of some sailors mixing their food scraps with general trash out of meanness.

In Hong Kong, he was docked for a week at a time. Early tensions were beginning to heat up between North and South Korea and Earl asked locals which side they would support if war would break out, and they answered, "Whoever feeds us the most."

With the struggling economy there, he found great deals on business suits. He ordered three Herringbone suits and prepaid at the cost of 25 dollars, but once again, due to the fast pace Navy life, he left port before he could pick them up.

Once in Hong Kong, Earl crossed the border into Kowloon, China, walking across a bridge over the Shenzhen River. He recalled something in Kowloon that was unknown to Americans: executions by shooting were being performed on the busy streets as people walked by in the middle of the day.

Italy was one of the Axis powers until her surrender in September 1943, and the country's economy was devastated by the war. Earl remembered visiting Naples and finding it difficult to acquire simple things like soap and, most importantly, people were also starving. Still, he enjoyed the rich history of Italy and especially the lost city of Pompeii near Naples. He spent a day visiting the ruins of the city, where volcanic ash covered citizens, preserving their bodies.

Earl ported in England many times, largely before the United States entered into the war in Europe and after the war. He ported in and out of the towns of South Hampton, and nearby Bristol and Avonmouth, spending five to six days per trip. He never made it to London, just as he never visited Paris when he ported in Cherbourg. He always worried the ship would leave without him. He would occasionally set out on a train, but always turned back.

After the war, porting in the English towns, he would occasionally go out for a beer. His early visits were both difficult and comical as he tried to understand the accents of people, as well as the many cultural differences.

"I'd go out to a pub and ask for a beer," he recalled, "and the bartender would ask, 'arf and arf.' I didn't understand what he meant at first." It was slang for half and half, for proportions of a lighter beer and dark ale beer served.

He once ordered a sandwich and the waiter brought back a bean sandwich. "I was a little angry and I wanted him to return it. The waiter said that is what they served as a sandwich over there, I just wanted a normal sandwich," Earl explained, laughing at the memory.

The *Buck* became famous for something other than military involvement. While docked at San Pedro and Long Beach Harbors in Los Angeles, they served as a setting for a movie called *The Skipper Surprised his Wife.*

The two weeks of scenes were filmed at dock and while the ship came into port from a short-distance run out to sea, as well as with the crew still on board. Earl mingled with some of the movie crew and actors while it was filmed.

The movie, The Skipper Surprised His Wife

CHAPTER TWENTY-THREE

U.S. AIR FORCE: PHILIPPINES

After another try at civilian life, Earl decided to join the newly created U.S. Air Force at Fort Knox, Kentucky, which allowed him to spend more time with his family.

Earl had also grown weary of being on the water, a feeling that continued through his life; he didn't like to be on any lake, river, or ocean even for recreation. At one point he received orders to return to the Navy. He was in two branches of service at the same time and required a Navy officer to release him from his Navy duty.

"I got chewed out by the draft board after I got out of the Navy because I didn't sign up again," he recalled. I was already in the Air Force and I got orders to report to San Diego 12th Naval District ASAP. The Navy assumed I would re-sign, and there was some delayed communication about my discharge up at Great Lakes. I told them my intent was to join the Air Force because of my family."

In the Air Force Earl became a tech sergeant and was stationed at Fort Knox for a few months before moving to Standiford Field, the commercial airport in Louisville, after the two bases traded air fields. Penny and the kids came to stay for a brief period, with Montee and Jim excited to spend time in Louisville with their Grandma and Grandpa Smith.

During the short stay at Standiford, Earl flew in a C-47 out to San Diego with a colonel, who was gaining his flight time. He'd then go up to

Los Angeles to see Penny and the kids after they had left Louisville. "The Colonel had a young grandson in San Diego; he wanted to fly out to see him and my family was out there too," Earl said. "Some of those other guys would go down to Biloxi and sit on the beach for four days just by getting their flight time. They got paid the whole time, too."

Earl's military assignment in Kentucky was short-lived and he was again uprooted and separated from his family. He got orders to relieve a man in South Korea for two weeks and then he was to be sent to the Philippines for 18 months.

"I never knew where I was going until I got there." he said. "I just knew [it was] the Far East. They didn't tell me a whole lot. Penny and the kids were going to come to Kentucky and live while I was stationed there. I planned to be in Louisville longer than that, but it all changed."

Earl, as a Master Sergeant, on his bunk in the Philippines

In the Philippines, Earl was stationed at Clark Field Air Force Base on Luzon Island near Angeles City in the province of Pampanga. He worked in air frame repair as part of the maintenance department and was in charge of repairing everything on the plane except the engine and hydraulics. Earl and his 50-man crew were a support outfit for the repairing of South Korean military planes. Some members of his crew were Filipino.

"Things were more relaxed there," he said. "I was an officer and allowed everyone to call me Smitty, unless a higher ranking officer was present. The Filipinos were good workers, worked hard and steady in the shop." He and his department helped rebuild a C-47 military plane, and when they were done, the captain would fly it out to different places every weekend, taking others along just for fun.

Earl remembered a trip to the town of Zamboanga, in the very extreme southern part of the Philippines. He recalled it being known to sailors as the home of the tailless monkeys. They may have been there, but more likely this notion came from the title of a 1907 song that U.S. sailors would sing in the Pacific during WWII. When Earl landed in Zamboanga, he recalled the runway being very rough and the weeds so high, they clipped the wings on the plane.

Because he was head of the maintenance department, Earl was contacted by an on base doctor who wanted to help a young local girl born with scoliosis. He and the doctor used a clothing store mannequin to help fit and form a spinal brace from Plexiglass material. Earl created the brace, using leather strapping to help it support her properly.

Earl's rebuilt C-47

While Earl was stationed in the Philippines, there was a strong earthquake, something unfamiliar to him, since he grew up in Kentucky and spent most of his military career on the open seas. Though he did once experience a small earthquake while he stayed in a San Francisco hotel, it was nothing like this.

"We all ran out of the hangar we were in," he said. "I saw the power lines shake and the ground began to feel like Jello. It was strong enough to cause some damage." The exact magnitude was unknown, but the area had periodic volcanic activity, which may have created the tremors.

Earl interacted with the locals, including native pygmies who lived in villages just outside the base. They were quite small in stature— the average adult was much shorter than the average American. They typically wore a traditional cloth or animal skin as a wraparound skirt or G-string. They spoke English well and were paid to help guard the base. It was 22 miles around Clark Field. Pygmies were known as marksmen who could hit precise targets with bows and arrows.

Earl recalled visiting the villages and befriending a very old man with tough weathered skin; he was barely over four feet tall and wore an animal skin G-string covering. The man picked a distant target and used his hand-made bow and arrow to easily hit it on the mark without difficulty. After seeing that, Earl thought the base was well protected.

He respected the Filipinos and thought they didn't receive the recognition they deserved for their help during the war, particularly the guerilla fighters. Many Filipinos were placed in prisoner of war camps when they were captured during the Japanese invasion. Earl later became good friends with a man from Colorado named Tripp who had been imprisoned by the Japanese. Tripp spoke of seeing many Filipinos beheaded by the Japanese with long sabers. The Japanese often forced American prisoners of war to watch these executions as a scare tactic.

Clark Field Air Force Base was three miles from Angeles City; each was located in the flatlands between Mount Arayat and Mount Pinatubo, an active volcano. Men stationed there had to be back on base by 10 p.m. because of what Earl called the disruptive and dangerous Filipino outlaws who lived in the mountains. They were known to the locals as the Aeta/ Ita people or tribe, but the G.I.s knew them as "huckabullahops" and they were most dangerous at night. The curfew was set to account for the time it took them to come down from the mountains into town at dusk.

The huckabullahops were similar to the pygmies in appearance and dress, but they were a little taller and far more violent. Earl recalled being in a tavern with other G.I.s during the daytime when members of the Aeta tribe came down and shot at the windows which sent the Americans diving to the ground and turning over tables for protection. The tribe was known to shoot at American military vehicles as well and they once shot and killed two G.I.s and two Filipino women, leaving their bodies in the hot sun as an example. Earl recalled the horrific smell of the scene.

Even with the danger in Angeles City, some G.I.s still went to town to hang out. A beer was only 25 cents, but many didn't have enough money to buy a drink. Ever the businessman, Earl became a loan shark, loaning money to the guys so they could go to town. His terms: five dollars loaned and a dollar in interest. "Some of those guys in my squadron couldn't move until I moved," Earl said. "They couldn't go to town until they got money from me. It eventually got old always chasing people down for my money though."

Loans
Hardy (LOAN) pd 35.00
Allen (car plates) 8.00
Mickey (LOAN) 2.00
Bill & Archie (LOAN) 35.00
Bill & Archie (DWI) 127 55
Sonny pd 10.00
Findlay pd 6 50
Howerton 13.28
Porter
Velma (LOAN) 10.00
Tarver (LOAN 20 00
Allen (car) 300.00
Evans (41 Ford) pd 4/10 25.00
Porter (Loan 5 00

Loan shark records

During that time the locals drove Jeeps that were left behind by the American military after the war. They converted them into taxi cabs and occasionally added cattle racks so they could haul more passengers. There was also bus transportation, Earl remembered those vehicles being called "Rabbits," old school buses that hauled hogs, sheep, and chickens in addition to people.

"They ran those Jeeps and buses bumper to bumper over there," Earl said. "When you rode the taxi cabs and had to go to the bathroom, you just tapped the driver on the shoulder. The women would just get off and face one way and the men would face another. That is just what they did; they had no problems either. It may have been just because of their culture, but I was told there wasn't any sexual assault in 50 years when they would do those things."

Civilian cars were rare in Filipino towns. Earl recalled G.I.s bringing vehicles over to sell because they could get four or five times more for them than they could in the United States. Earl remembered a G.I. bringing over a newly built black Buick that so impressed the locals because of its shiny color, that the G.I. made a big profit with the sale.

"I bought a stick-shift Crosley car off a soldier when I got over there," Earl said. "They were the same company that made iceboxes and radios back in the states. One night after being out in the town, we still had to get back to base by the 10 o'clock curfew. It was getting close to curfew and many of the guys were still out drinking and stranded. I drove that little Crosley with 10 guys in it, hanging on the sides and standing on the bumpers speeding to get back to base. I lost one guy on a sharp turn and had to put it in reverse and go back. I just put him on the roof and made it in." Earl kept the memories, but gave the car to another G.I. when he left.

Earl got scared once when he was out in the Filipino jungle with a few fellow soldiers and came into contact with a 15-foot black King Cobra. The enormous snake dropped on the back of a soldier as they cut through the boom grass of the jungle. The soldier turned to see the snake at eye level. He whacked it with a machete, but later the snake was found alive while being transported to the snake doctor on base. Earl was unsure about what a snake doctor really did, but he knew they were usually American G.I.s in charge of the snake ward. Due to the numerous venomous snakes in the country, they may have worked on proper snake identification and extracting venom for creating anti-venom drugs.

"The snake was being transported in the back of a 12-ton Army truck with a few other guys stationed there. I watched them start to drive off." Earl said. "It was both scary and hysterical to see when the sun started getting hot and warming up that snake and he began to move, then trying to bring his head up and spread out his neck. Those guys jumped out of that truck, as fast as they could, even as it went down the road. I think the driver even stopped and jumped out. I guess he was only knocked out." Earl had a good laugh at that memory.

G.I.s lived four to a room and one of Earl's roommates and friends was a staff sergeant named Fennell. Fennell was a former POW of the Philippines Bataan Death March and Camp O'Donnell. The Death March began on April 9, 1942, when the Japanese forced 75,000 American and Filipino POW's to march for six days 80 miles north to Camp O'Donnell where they were held. Some 10,000 POW's died along the way, and many were severely beaten. Earl recalled his friend not speaking too much about the march, but he did tell Earl one story. Gold was common in dentistry at the time and Earl remembered being told of the Japanese using the butt of their rifle, knocking out and collecting gold teeth or gold fillings if they were spotted in a G.I.'s mouth.

Earl and Fennell had been roommates for a year when Fennell became ill and developed a fever. He was worsening as the day went on and asked Earl to take him to the base hospital. Earl did, and Fennell asked him to return to the barracks for his personal items.

When Earl got back to the hospital, he knocked on the door to hand them over. A doctor opened and after a long pause and deep breath said, "He won't be needing those; he just died." Fennell had passed during the short time that Earl was gone. He never knew the cause of death and was only told Fennell had a very high fever. Earl thought it was complications from polio. A large Catholic funeral for him was held on base.

Chapter Twenty-four

AS LOW AS A MAN CAN GO

The long stints away from home took a toll on his marriage. It was while Earl was in the Philippines that problems in his marriage surfaced, though he didn't quite realize it until he received divorce papers. He admitted covering his eyes to earlier problems. Penny didn't show up for two port calls to come down to the Philippines, which led to long, argumentative phone conversations.

"I was called in for questioning after Penny missed that second port call," Earl said. "They wanted to know what was going on. I told them I was 6,000 miles from home and I just didn't know what was going on. I finally just told them it was due to a family illness. I had to tell them something."

When he returned to Los Angeles after completing his tour, Earl learned that Penny had moved to Granada Hills. He went to the house one night and found her with another man, with whom Earl assumed she was living. Later, he learned that the man, who was much larger than Earl, initially had hid under the bed when Earl showed up. It turned out that while Earl was out of the country, Penny began dating someone she met while working at a local aircraft manufacturing company.

"She told me to come back the next day so I could see my kids," he said. "There was no motel and I was upset, so I walked the streets all night. I came back the next day and was able to spend a few hours with them. I was still upset and I asked my daughter, who was around nine years old at the time, if her mom and that man were sharing the same bed together. Penny found out what I had asked."

Penny filed a restraining order, asserting he was harassing the children stemming from that question. Earl found out when he returned to pick them up for another visit a few days later.

"I came back and this guy came out of the house and approached me," he said. "I brought my fists up because I didn't know who he was and things had gotten pretty tense then. He asked if I was James Earl Smith. He then touched me once; that was all they had to do. He said, 'You have been served.'"

Earl was angry but realized he had a 15-year military career to think about, which he could not jeopardize. When Earl had left for the Philippines, he had 10,000 dollars in savings, a house, furniture that was paid for, and three cars. He returned with nothing. Later, he learned the money he sent from the Philippines was not going to care of his children, but to fund Penny's new single lifestyle.

"She put me as low as a man can go," Earl said with anger in his voice. "She put me underneath cigarette butts in the gutter and then rolled me. My ambition was to be a good family man and a good father. She robbed me of that."

Earl determined the marriage was un-repairable and hired an attorney who said he would take care of everything and suggested Earl head back to Louisville to cool off.

Earl had no way home to Louisville and lacked the money, so he answered an ad in the *Los Angeles Times* to share expenses on a cross-country drive. He had once owned two Chevy convertibles and another automobile he called a work car, but Penny sold them or had given them away. So Earl left L.A. with three college students who were returning to Connecticut after spring break. They asked if Earl would drive through the Rocky Mountains as part of the deal and charged him 20 dollars for the ride home; they dropped him at his parents' doorstep.

He soon took a bus to Detroit after hearing he could get a good deal on a car. He bought a used green two-door 1941 Hudson Hornet. That wasn't his only time in Detroit. A few months later, he returned in that Hudson with a crew of Carl, and brothers-in-law Tommy and Wilbur Allen.

"Those guys wanted me to take them up there a few months after I bought that Hudson," Earl said, smiling. "Tommy went up there with me because of the good deals, but he told me he didn't have any money. Then he saw one he liked and just pulled the money right out of his shoe to pay. I told them, 'He is from the country. We do things a little different.'"

Earl's children, Montee and Jim, circa 1950

After Earl bought his new car, he drove it home from Detroit and then made the 2,000 mile journey to Los Angeles, in an effort to see his children. It failed, as did two more attempts within a 36-day stretch. He saw his children one time in 27 months and he learned Penny was moving around and hiding the children. Mostly, they stayed with Penny's sister and her husband. Earl was determined to locate them and searched so frantically that he once saw a boy crossing the street and thought it was his son, Jim. Earl wanted to be sure his children knew he did not desert them. He eventually hired a private investigator, who located them.

Earl showed up at Penny's house unannounced one day, but the children were quickly sent to the back of the house and told to hide under the bed. Penny told Earl they were not there. The kids disobeyed their mom's orders and peeked out the window to see their dad on their doorstep, then walking up and down the sidewalk, upset. Earl knew he was being lied to.

As he searched for his children, his Los Angeles attorney dragged his feet on the divorce and seemed to be taking advantage of Earl. At one point, he stopped responding to Earl's many letters regarding the case's status.

In a letter to the attorney, a copy of which was found in Earl's lock box after his death, he wrote: "I know you are a very busy man. Did you get the other letters and the 175 dollars I sent? This process is going so slow, I just want this [divorce] to be over so I can see my kids."

Earl was assigned to Amarillo Air Force Base in Texas and was eager to get the legal right to visit his children; he contacted an attorney in Amarillo to take over the case. When Earl requested a transfer of his files, he then received word that his first attorney had died. Earl lost all of the money he'd paid, plus any progress on the case.

Fighting a losing battle in California, Earl filed suit in Texas and was finally granted a divorce. He sued for custody of the children, and the state of Texas granted custody to Earl and his parents, but California did not recognize the ruling. This incident angered Penny and furthered damaged their relationship, as in evidence by her letter to Earl around Christmas during the divorce process.

"The children received the watches," Penny wrote. "They thought they were nice and said 'thanks.' Maybe someday you will wise-up that we don't care if we ever see you again; the way you have done by them. I doubt if they ever will want to see you again. Jim don't even remember you and Montee thinks you are square. You made it that way. Not me. You should of stopped and thought of your children's welfare instead of how

I broke your little heart. I hope you drop dead. So we won't be seeing you for a long time, Mr. Smith."

Earl reflected back on the situation. "I was assigned to Texas, but I did like the Philippines. I had to try to take care of the situation at home. Then, I felt I had nothing here for me in the States. I wanted to go back there [the Philippines], but there were no openings."

Penny ended up with much of what he believed he worked for, including his kids. "I would have fought it more if I was a civilian, so she wouldn't have cleaned me out," Earl said. "My lawyer was dragging his feet, but still, if he hadn't died, things would have been much better."

After the divorce, living in Texas, Earl constantly thought about his two children in Los Angeles. Things were even more strained with Penny, which made visitation extremely difficult. Earl, using military leave, made several unsuccessful trips to see them. At Christmas time the following year, showing up unannounced, Earl saw his children. Using some persuasion on Penny, he took them down to Bill's house in San Diego for three days, then back to L.A. He returned to Texas and didn't see them again for two years.

CHAPTER TWENTY-FIVE

HARD TIMES IN AMARILLO

The divorce led Earl into a dark period of fighting and drinking, which lasted four years. Earl had never taken a drink until the Navy, but now his drinking was excessive. Still, working day shift on base, he never neglected his military duties, but admitted sometimes coming close. He also operated a modest, filling station, Cities Service Company, located on Highway 60 in Amarillo. The concrete block station changed oil and transmission fluid, but he had no grease racks or garage, so vehicles had to be jacked up outside. It had six full-service gas pumps, and at retail cost, he sold regular gasoline just under 20 cents per gallon. (Earl reflected on how gas prices had more than doubled, even then. In 1939, for example, while on leave from the *Argonne* in L.A., he recalled filling up his Model A ten gallon tank for less than a dollar.)

Experiencing rough times made Earl even more eager to help others in tough situations. Once a semi-truck driver came in for gas, explaining he lost his company gas card. He was driving on fumes and needed 100 gallons to finish carrying his load west. Other stations had sent him away, but Earl let him gas up on only a handshake. As the man promised, a week later Earl received full payment and a thank you note from the trucking company addressed only to the nice man. For Earl's generosity, the company began filling up exclusively at the nice man's station when they passed through Amarillo.

Earl sold the filling station after less than a year and bought a bar, the 66 Drive Inn, not far from base on six acres along historic Route 66 in Amarillo. The road, known as one of the original U.S. highways, ran from L.A. to Chicago. The base helped make the bar a popular G.I. hang out and the highway helped increase Earl's civilian customers, but he was in no position to keep track of the business.

Earl had a lot of trouble with the law during this period and was arrested several times. Even in civilian clothes, G.I.s were recognizable from their required bumper stickers. Once Earl was driving back to base, from a nearby town, and despite the Amarillo Air Force Base sticker on his car, he was pulled over. The police said it was for driving too slow, but really it was actually a set up—to attempt to arrest him for being intoxicated.

Had he been waved through the gate at base, he could not have been stopped. In his Hornet, he knew he could have outrun the cop, and he regretted not doing so after he found out what lay ahead.

After Earl and his roommate Rudolph were stopped, Earl was arrested for suspicion of driving under the influence. His car was impounded, and Rudolph returned to base.

The city officer put Earl in the back seat of the police cruiser and turned up the heat, then shoved him when he tried to roll down the window. He assumed Earl had been drinking and was trying to make him sick on that warm fall day. But this time Earl had not been drinking.

"I told him if you think you are going to make me sick by turning up the heat, you got another thing coming," Earl said. "Me and Rudolph had just bought a loaf of bread and some bologna and were eating. That's it."

At the jail, the nurse who drew his blood told him it was a false arrest, a racket the police had been running on G.I.s. The blood test eventually turned out negative, but it had to be mailed to Austin, the state capital, which took eight to ten days. A tech sergeant who had been jailed for eight days, suggested Earl plead guilty. He paid a $127.50 fine and got released.

The police officer kept Earl's driver's license. At the impound lot, the parking attendant, told Earl he was railroaded and that the officer had been rolling G.I.s. Earl realized he was being followed by a detective and figured he would be pulled over if he drove, so he called some friends to drive him back to base. He got a three-day pass, waited until nightfall and snuck out, driving through nearby Oklahoma toward Louisville, 16 hours away, where he got a Kentucky driver's license.

"That sheriff didn't like me and any other G.I.," Earl said. "His exact words, we were all 'sons of bitches.'" Earl later went back just to aggravate him. "I was like a crazy teenager. He would find out I was in town and come after me. I'd outrun him in that car of mine, then hit the highway and head back. One time I almost hit a rock fence doing it, but it was worth it."

That was Earl's first arrest. His second came after he and his G.I. roomate, Brown, tried to break up a domestic dispute one early evening between an acquaintance of Earl and her husband, whose name was Sullivan. She briefly had worked at Earl's filling station. She ran a filling station with Sullivan and a parking lot next to the base's back gate. The parking was for soldiers without car insurance who weren't allowed to park on base. Earl recalled parking there for a short time.

Trying to break up the fight, Earl was thrown into a car and cut his head. When the police came, he and Brown were arrested for disorderly conduct. It was right after their shift, and it drew attention because both were still in their uniform. Earl had just taken off his work boots and socks and was in his bare feet. When the police came, he and Brown were arrested for disorderly conduct. They spent the night in jail, paid a ten dollar fine and were released. They weren't roommates long after that and both went their separate ways. Earl had a .32 Mauser pistol stolen around that time. Later, he sadly learned that Brown had committed suicide using that same gun.

The third arrest came in Clarendon, Texas, 50 miles below Amarillo, after a man sideswiped Earl and ran him off the road in the late afternoon, almost causing him to wreck. It was Sullivan.

Sullivan was husky, a head taller than Earl, and a well-known man from Clarendon. He was also known to run people off the road just to see how close he could get, but this time he made it personal. He believed

Earl was having an affair with his wife, whom he hadn't seen much of since the fight.

Earl fought with Sullivan along the highway and they rolled down the side of the road. Earl recalled being roughed up, but in the end, getting the best of Sullivan. A passing Greyhound bus driver got out and stopped the fight, and the town sheriff stopped by. He said he didn't like G.I.s, called Earl a dirty S.O.B and arrested him, letting the cop's friend Sullivan go. At the police station, the sheriff even threatened to pistol whip Earl, but the sheriff's wife who worked there stuck up for him and told her husband he didn't deserve that. Earl was released without being charged. There was little evidence and the sheriff never saw them fighting.

Fortunately, Earl had a friend living nearby and went to his house after he was released. The friend said that Sullivan, his brother-in-law, Shorty, and another man were waiting in the parking lot near his car. From the upstairs window, Earl saw them waiting on the sidewalk. He called a friend in Amarillo, and asked him to go to the 66 Drive Inn and get some friends. A few hours later, five men arrived with chains, crowbars and pipes. Earl walked out with his friends, got into a vehicle and drove straight back to Amarillo.

"I walked out like Al Capone. They didn't even try to move an inch. It was killing them," Earl said smiling. "We drove away without any problem."

Though he owned a bar in Amarillo, Earl hung out in other bars, and talked to the owners, who were all friends in the community. A few days after his most recent arrest, he was drinking a beer in the Wagon Wheel Inn. He spoke to the owner briefly and got ready to leave. On his way to the door, he saw Shorty sitting in a booth with a friend. He had been harassing and stalking Earl since the fight with his brother-in-law. Shorty jumped up, words were spoken, and Shorty broke a beer bottle on the counter and gestured as if he was going to cut Earl.

Earl always said he tried not to swear, but he was tired of this matter, which seemed to linger. He got angry and pointed his finger in Shorty's face, telling him if he moved he would "tear his (expletive) damn head off." Shorty got the picture, put down the broken bottle and left, never to be seen again. Weeks later, Sullivan came into Earl's bar looking for him, but he wasn't there. Sullivan told the waitress to thank him for what he did, because he was now divorced. Earl knew nothing had occurred, but he was glad this guy might disappear now.

"Looking back at that time after my divorce, it was a rough patch that I wouldn't want to go through again," he admitted. "It was a dangerous time. I just didn't care. I had more fun in Amarillo because of the way I was feeling, than I could think about in California or any other place. After losing my family, I just didn't care about anything anymore."

Earl's life had grown busy and chaotic, but he couldn't neglect his military duties, though he was concerned how his arrests might affect how the Air Force viewed him. Earl ran the base's maintenance department which included teaching the class instructors at the on-base technical school.

As he had done in the Philippines, he led the effort to rebuild a C-47. The squadron commander would take them up in that rebuilt plane and fly them to different places in the U.S., sometimes even out of the country to places like Hong Kong.

Earl never got in trouble in the military, but he saw many soldiers receive a court-martial. He sat on a court-martial once in the Navy; he recalled it as a 10-to-12 man jury to determine a sailor's punishment. But in the Air Force, he once had to go and retrieve G.I.s who were court-martialed for being AWOL.

He drove from Amarillo to Scott Air Force Base near St. Louis to pick up two G.I.s who were detained there. They both had gone to visit family and were captured in their home town. One had a sick family member and had requested emergency leave through the Red Cross, normal procedure at the time, but his request had been denied.

"I drove up there and I told them, 'You are not prisoners.' I didn't handcuff them," Earl recalled. "I wanted them not to try and pull anything in return. I was strapped with a side-arm. When we stopped to eat, I treated them like regular guys. We got back, and I found out the one boy had ran away again."

Chapter Twenty-six

THE ORCHID

Marion Anita Dye, circa 1940

Things soon changed for Earl because that spring following his final arrest, he met Marion Anita Dye, who would become his second wife. He called her the Orchid. He called Penny "Rose" and Marion "Orchid" based upon a favorite song and also his love for Marion. The song "Overlooked an Orchid (While Searching for a Rose)," as Earl said, "...just summed it all up."

Marion was from North Little Rock, Arkansas, and had parents who divorced when she was very young. Her father, Lloyd Dye, a former WWI male nurse and medic, owned a small store where he started out selling comic books and popcorn, and that grew into a clothes and shoe store. He had another side business that was more profitable—back room gambling. He also sold the popcorn on passenger trains and buses, and attained the name "Popcorn Pete." Her mother, born Velma Peck, had an 8th grade education and worked many jobs, but notably, for a well-known retail clothing store and insurance company.

Marion, a very outgoing and pretty red-head, was previously divorced and already had children of her own. She came to Texas to visit her younger sister Catherine that summer, who was stricken with Bright's [kidney] disease. Marion then decided to stay because of the disease's advancement. Catherine was in Amarillo because her husband was also stationed at the base. She eventually succumbed to the disease after leaving Amarillo.

Marion, who was very hard working, had previous experience owning and running a restaurant in Little Rock, Arkansas, serving plate lunches. She also had a family history in the restaurant business, as her maternal grandparents owned a BBQ restaurant in Little Rock.

Catherine's husband and Earl were friends, and he knew Earl was looking for someone to work at his bar, so Marion walked in looking for a job as a waitress. Earl's regular waitress had headed back to Alabama to tend to a family matter, and Earl knew he would be short on staff that night. He asked when she could start. She said "Do you have an apron?" Earl was required by a city ordinance at the bar to have what he called "Eats" when serving alcohol, so Marion would always have stew sandwiches and mountain oysters available.

Earl and Marion both soon realized they had experienced similar marital conditions and instantly felt a bond. Also, the patrons, who were mostly G.I.s, all loved her and the Orchid blossomed. Eventually she was running the place and had stolen his heart. They were eager to get married without delay, so they drove to Clovis, New Mexico, in the early winter of that year, and had a small chapel ceremony.

Earl always credits Marion for helping him become a better man and saving his life. He would try to show his love over the years, and one way was by leaving love poems on the kitchen table for her to wake up to.

I get up in the morning the house is so cold
I look outside and its zero and below
I think back at the times when I was a lad
All these chores that fell upon my dad
Now I am trying to fill Dad's shoes
I do all these chores while the family snooze
It is hard to get started on a cold dreary day
But you have to do it to expect any pay
At least the day has gone by and I head for home
To be greeted by a warm family and a home sweet home

Dad

"Marion took my eyes when I first seen her, she was so pretty," Earl said smiling and reflecting back, as it appears one single memory seemed to make everything that ever was bad, good again. "I still remember the blue dress she was wearing; it was a little low cut. She changed my life for the better. I was living pretty rough and just emotionally tired at that time, and she got me back on the right path. She has always been my inspiration; we've had so many happy years together."

Together, Earl and Marion raised six children as part of their combined family: Velma Jane, Ricky Lee, Tina Marie, Patricia Ann, Dorothy Anita Bolton, and James Marion Bolton.

Because of his heavy drinking, and now with children at home he considered his own, Marion asked Earl to sell the bar and he did. He had no particular fondness for that type of business and admitted he rarely checked the register or counted the money. As long as he kept his head above water, he simply didn't care, though he thought employees had their hands in the cash register.

Earl returned to the filling station business by leasing a building from Gulf Oil and selling supplies. This filling station, better equipped than the first, was located in Panhandle, Texas, 24 miles northeast from Amarillo. The station contained a garage, grease rack, a wash rack, and several full service pumps. He owned a house between the station and base along with a 300 head hog farm next to it. Life for him began to calm down and Earl ran the station a few years until selling.

After learning he would have a deployment to France, he then, with the rank of master sergeant, decided to leave the Air Force and put in his retirement papers in the spring of 1958. Earl was simply tired of traveling, especially to France again.

The next G.I. in line—a man named Sowers—received Earl's orders which were changed from France to Spain. Earl had been close enough to Spain to hit it with a stone; he'd been through the Strait of Gibraltar, but never docked or stepped foot on Spain's soil.

"I was tired of traveling, but I would have stayed in if I knew I was going to be deployed to Spain," he said, laughing. "I just didn't want to go to France again." Earl retired from active military duty in November of 1958 after 21 years. He remained in the Air Force Reserves for an additional nine years, and, at one point, had standby orders for Vietnam.

Chapter Twenty-seven

CIVILIAN LIFE IN MARENGO

Retired and armed with a monthly pension and some savings, Earl returned to a civilian way of life. He quickly moved from Amarillo and settled on property in a small town, Marengo, in Southern Indiana, where he and his brother Carl went in together to purchase the land. They also went in together on another piece of property and Carl eventually moved just east of Marengo.

"I retired at the very end of November and we stayed one night in Little Rock, Arkansas, to see Marion's family and moved to Indiana on December 2nd," Earl recalled. "I had been separated from my family in Louisville so much while in the Navy, I wanted to be close, but not in the city." Marengo was a little less than an hour driving distance from Louisville. "I helped buy it and moved in, after only being to the town twice."

He originally planned to farm, but was ill prepared to be a civilian or a farmer. In the military, he was taught a lot, but being a farmer was something the armed forces didn't teach.

The farm they lived on sat up on a hill and water was pumped to the house from a spring nearby. During one especially lean stretch, he shot birds to feed his family. "It was hard when we first moved up here. I borrowed 12 dollars from Dad just to buy groceries and it has always bothered me that I never paid him back before he died."

Earl, after less than a year after moving to Marengo, had other problems—more trouble with Penny. The Crawford County sheriff came to notify Earl that legal actions had been filed against him along with the sheriff handing over the California court issued document. The complaints surrounded the custody of their children and neglect of reasonable support for them. Penny was requesting a substantial increase in child support.

"I had been paying the same amount for years," Earl said, "and then she wanted more." He asked for permission to take a bath first; the Crawford County sheriff knew Earl and trusted he would come to the County's Attorney's office later. In a short amount of time, Earl was able to get representation from a well-known area attorney who told him not to go and let him take care of it, but Earl went. He went anyway because of the frustration of remembering how his divorce process went.

His attorney responded Plea and Abatement to the complaints, a pleading where the defendant does not object to the claims, but objects to its form or time. In the end, Earl didn't have to pay any extra child support due to what he thinks was the result of the plea and the current laws between the two states.

"I paid my attorney 125 dollars for basically two words and I didn't understand what it all meant, but I was glad it was over," he said. "I wanted my kids taken care of and I had always paid the child support amount that we agreed on."

Old Jim, the donkey, 1960
Front to back, Rick, Tina, and Patsy

Though he had little money during his early years in Marengo, Earl was able to surprise his children one Christmas, as well as other times. He bought a donkey from his cousin Pearl, who lived in Illinois. He hid the donkey, which had just come from Mexico, in the basement. When the kids came down the stairs on Christmas morning and saw him, they began screaming from excitement. Old Jim, as the donkey became known, came to be the farm's best attribute, handling farm work and also letting the kids climb all over him without complaint. Still fondly remembered, Old Jim loved to eat candy, but did not like the family dog.

Earl also bought a three-year-old pony named Tony, which he had for 34 years. He'd first tried to buy Tony at an auction, but he was outbid. Earl realized the man didn't really need the pony and with some persuading and an additional five dollars, bought him. Tony then became part of the family.

Earl eventually gave up on the idea of farming full time and began to work for the Louisville Board of Education in the maintenance department. The school system included 77 schools. He worked in Louisville for four years, and recalled seeing a young boxer near his school named Cassius Clay multiple times shadow boxing while running down Shawnee Parkway. This was before Clay won the Gold medal in the 1960 Olympics, and well before he converted to Islam and changed his name to Muhammad Ali.

Earl left that job and got another in Marengo working as a custodian for the Marengo School Corporation. His work was confined to a small campus of two school buildings (with part of one being the gym) that housed children in grades 1-12.

After six years, Marion was eager to move from the 298-acre farm into the Marengo city limits. Earl, with a job at the school, thought that it made sense for the family, and decided to move to a new house nearby. Working at the school became a family affair. Earl paid his children a few dollars a week to help out. His youngest son, Rick, saved enough to buy a mini-bike.

Earl eventually left the school corporation to work as a mail carrier for the U.S. Post Office in Marengo. He held that job for 13 years until he reached retirement age.

Upon his retirement, Earl and Marion managed to travel and visit many places throughout the United States, Canada, and Mexico. Earl found the west, including the Rocky Mountains in Colorado, especially beautiful and thought that everyone, particularly his grandchildren should experience it. Earl and Marion ventured to the bright lights of Las Vegas, and he remembered the late 1940s, when Las Vegas was just another desert town he passed en route to Los Angeles. Also, he enjoyed the good times at the New Orleans Mardi Gras.

Earl in Juarez, Mexico, 1997

Earl would frequent the western rodeos, especially in Cheyenne, Wyoming. He was known to talk to anybody and once, with his trademark sense of humor, Earl started a conversation with the musician, Jimmy Dean at a Lubbock, Texas, rodeo; Dean was to perform after the event. Dean had some country hits, such as "Big Bad John," before founding the Jimmy Dean Sausage Company.

"I was excited to talk to him," Earl said, laughing and admitting to a little white lie. "I told him I loved his sausage and I ate it every morning. I had never even tasted it before."

Chapter Twenty-eight

BUSINESS ADVENTURES

Through the years, Earl and Marion started several businesses that became local institutions in and around Marengo where they lived some 40 years after relocating from Texas. The businesses included two grocery stores, a small trucking business, a drive-in restaurant, and a furniture store. He thought they were good investments, where he could earn extra money and better himself and he thought Marengo could benefit as well.

The seasonal restaurant, Smitty's Place, specialized in a great variety of ice cream flavors, and was in business for about three years. It became a small high-school hang out and place to stop after a local baseball game or on the way back from the nearby Patoka Lake for a "Smitty's Hot Diggity" (foot-long hot dog) and a scoop of orange sherbet ice cream.

The downtown Marengo grocery store, named Smitty's Market, was family-run, with free delivery that included helping disabled customers put away groceries. Earl's teenage grandson, Jacob, worked there during high school and would often pour out a customer's milk into a special container because of her arthritic hands.

"I wanted to invest in something that helped the community," Earl said. "I think I did. I was hoping for it to be a good investment, too." Earl eventually had to close the doors of the store. It did help the community, but turned out not to be a good financial investment.

Then there was S & S Furniture Store, a prominent family business they owned and operated for 31 years. S & S had a few initial locations, but eventually ended up in a former well-known dance hall called the Tip Top, which sat below the house.

The furniture store wasn't large, but was well-known in the community. Marion ran the business and handled the books, while Earl provided the labor. They specialized in top-of-the line living room and bed room furniture, appliances, and carpeting. Trying to aid the community, Earl and Marion adopted a very customer friendly policy, which had good and bad results. The credit policy was relaxed and simply relied on the customer's word. They charged no interest and offered free delivery.

Earl made deliveries in the family truck, covering a good part of surrounding Southern Indiana area and Louisville; he also made some trips to Arkansas and Alabama.

Customers were to pay what they could; unfortunately, some took advantage of the situation with hard luck stories. Once, a woman bought several items, then turned around and filed bankruptcy. Many made payments for a while, but stopped before paying in full. The credit debts eventually began to add up over time.

Not everyone was a poor risk. The store had many good customers who stayed true to their word, paying what they could little by little until their balance reached zero. Many customers were just starting out in life, living on their own for the first time, or just-married. They often had little money and remained eternally grateful for the help Earl and Marion offered, saying they never would have had anything starting out if it weren't for their kindness. Because of Earl and Marion's age and eagerness to officially retire, the S & S Furniture Store was finally closed.

CHAPTER TWENTY-NINE

REMEMBERING PEARL HARBOR AND WWII

In May 2001, after Hollywood made a version of the attack on Pearl Harbor, Earl experienced memories that he hadn't thought of for many years. He'd seen other Pearl Harbor movies, but this one gave him nightmares about the destruction, after he'd gone many years without such a problem.

"That movie brought up some old left-over memories, he said. "In my dreams I saw guys in the water covered in oil and burning. There was a lot of death and destruction that the movie had right, but there sure was no love story when I was there."

Earl realized the film, made in December 2001, was timed to coincide with the 60th anniversary of the attack, but everything was amplified by the September 11, 2001, terrorist attacks on New York and Washington D.C. Earl, like the rest of country, was astounded by those horrifying events, which brought back memories of the other unexpected attack that most Americans were now too young to recall.

"I hated to see this happening to us," he said, "and again on American soil. We didn't know who the enemy was this time. It wasn't anybody's military."

In December 1991, Jim and Marion traveled to Hawaii for the 50th anniversary in remembrance of the attack on Pearl Harbor. He enjoyed the visit, but not as much as the 60th anniversary he and his family celebrated in Fredericksburg, Texas, outside San Antonio. That was early December 2001, with the airports on very high alert, because of the 9/11 attacks. Many of Earl's family members boarded planes from Louisville and California and headed to Texas to commemorate the first attack on the American homeland; Fredericksburg was the home of Admiral Nimitz and the site of the Admiral Nimitz Historical Center, Nimitz Museum, and George H.W. Bush Gallery of the National Museum of the Pacific War.

Former President George H.W. Bush, a WWII veteran himself, spoke to honor survivors as well as those who perished. Earl visited the museum where he ran into and had a brief conversation with the actor and former WWII marine, Cliff Robertson. Robertson, who won an Academy Award, was perhaps best known for the film, *PT 109,* in which he portrayed John F. Kennedy.

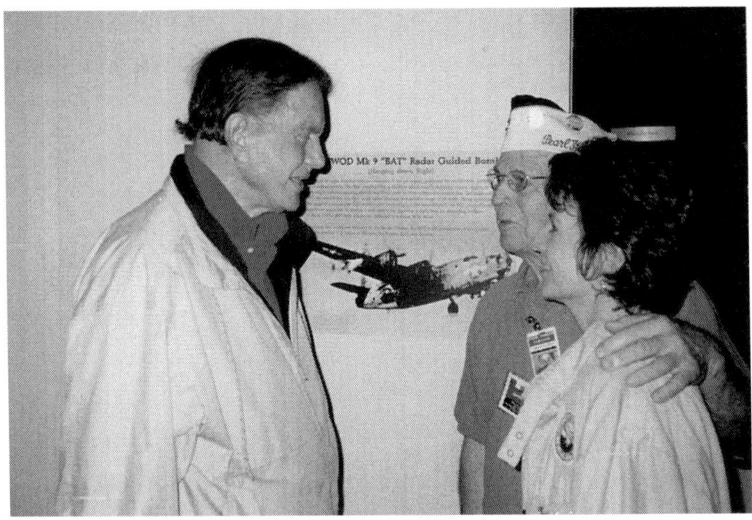

Earl and daughter Tina talking to actor Cliff Robertson, 2001

Through the years, Earl stayed involved in the Pearl Harbor Survivors of Kentucky Blue Grass Chapter and, along with the other members, he had been acknowledged in his local paper, Louisville's *Courier Journal,* and the local Louisville media as the Pearl Harbor anniversary rolled around. He and the other survivors had never before seen this type of celebration and gratitude.

The celebration also included local TV station crews with cameras rolling along, and with bystanders stopping and listening to old war stories like wide-eyed young children. Also, a parade through town was performed in their honor. Pearl Harbor survivors, who were physically able, were placed in the back of military trucks and driven in the parade while parade watchers saluted and said, "Thank you." Survivors who couldn't get into the truck were also graciously greeted and thanked.

Earl telling stories about the war with local reporters, 2001

"I loved that trip," Earl recalled with a smile. "It was so pleasant. I would do it over again and again. I have everything still photographed in my mind."

Later in life, when he and Marion were still able to travel, they were able to visit the WWII memorial in Washington, D.C., and see the tribute

Earl in back of military truck, greeting parade-goers in Fredericksburg, Texas, 2001

to those fought in the war and, to what was very close to Earl, the Pacific Theater. He was able to see in person plaques of him and his brothers placed on the wall of the Mount Soledad Veterans Memorial in San Diego. These memorials were two things he especially felt honored to see.

Mount Soledad Veterans Memorial honoring Earl and his brothers, with Carl top left, and Earl and Bill bottom row (left to right)

Pearl Harbor Memorial in Washington, D.C., 2004

CHAPTER THIRTY

A LOOK BACK

Earl was the last surviving Smith sibling. As he looked back over his days growing up, his military career, and his life afterwards, he always maintained he was shaped by his family's values.

"I had a wonderful and close family growing up; what one had, the other one was welcome to," he recalled. "We never had hard feelings toward each other. I'm glad I grew up that way. I never had a great desire to get away from home. I just didn't have any future; I had nothing. I had to go."

Family photo of Earl's mom, dad, and siblings (left to right) Nina, Ruth, Janie, Jim W. (center), Earl, Carl, and Bill

Earl had his own personal view of money and living since his early years. "I've been called stingy; I'm conservative," he said. "I've been called stingy because I don't buy everything that everybody wants. But when you think about it, I've had a rich life."

Earl was bothered for many years about what happened with his first marriage. "When it comes to my first two children, Montee and Jim, it is all in the open," he said. "I told them in person what all happened with their mother; they understand the situation. And I am so happy they do, because I never intended for it to go that way. When all that was going on they were never too far from my thoughts. I was always scared they would think I didn't love them or had deserted them."

He added: "Later, I do think I succeeded in being a family man and a good father that I wasn't before. Marion helped me to achieve all the things that I wanted out of life; she gave me a wonderful family that has given me so much joy and that I love very much."

Earl and Marion dancing at Pearl Harbor 60th anniversary, Fredericksburg tribute, 2001

When he was asked about WWII and the attack on Pearl Harbor, which was such a major event and turning point in his life, he continued to say: "God was good to me. He let me survive and come home. The heroes are the ones who didn't come home. Being a Pearl Harbor survivor is not something I advertised. I was there because I had to be, not because I wanted to. But I want to say something. I want to take my hat off to all veterans of all wars."

Earl with his childhood friend Sol, 2003

The Smith family, 2011. Front row: Earl and Marion,
Back row (left to right): Jane, Tina, Rick, Patsy, Jim, Montee, Dorothy
(not pictured: James Bolton)

Earl at Falls of Rough bridge months before his death, 2011

POSTSCRIPT

The reason for the book was to record one man's journey in a colorful and eventful life and beyond a few stories told and eventually forgotten after his death. Also, it is a dedication to him, his generation, all war veterans, and to his family. This was not written just in remembrance of James Earl Smith for those who were close to him, but in remembrance of all those who helped shape his life, so their children and grandchildren may also have lasting memories.

This book was created from the memory of a 90 year old man, James Earl Smith, or Earl, as he is known in the book. His reflection was mostly from a time that a majority of us don't know—his time. It is easy to see that many people he talked about had eventful lives and their own story to tell as well. Some may agree that details of them and all memories would have been more vivid if done many years prior to his reaching the age of 90. That may be true, but also it could be said that a person finally realizes his mortality and then becomes ready to tell his story openheartedly. James Earl Smith, opened up his heart and mind, and told his story.

Throughout the interviewing process and writing of this book, things would occur that came to foreshadow the end of Earl's long life. Penny Silk, his first wife and the mother of two of his children, died in Las Vegas of cancer. Earl had battled melanoma skin cancer throughout his later years, but then he was diagnosed with mesothelioma, a form of malignant cancer. This was a cancer that can be traced to his excessive exposure to asbestos, which was commonly on WWII Naval ships and in Navy yards during that time. Cancer, throughout Earl's life, was something he knew very well; it had taken the life of his father and each sibling.

The doctors told Earl's family that he had six months to live after his January 2011 diagnosis. In the early and middle part of his final days, he was able to visit with family and friends at home in modest comfort.

Earl could not leave home as the cancer progressed, but did receive a baptism performed in his bathtub. Once finished, Earl was left sitting in the tub for a few seconds with a smile and a sense of peace on his face. He would only respond "I have been needing to do that for a long time."

During his very last days, and bedridden, Earl seemed to have conversations with his dad and brothers more and more, as if he was still trying to relive and resolve earthly matters before he could move on. Then it seemed all was taken care of and he even came to know the day he would die. James Earl Smith passed away on June 10, 2011, and was given a full military honors burial for his contribution to preserving freedom in the United States and around the world.

Much has changed in the world since the Dec. 7, 1941, Japanese attack on Pearl Harbor and the United States entering WWII. The U.S. has seen other wars: Korea, Vietnam, and three wars in the Middle East. The entire globe has changed. Hawaii has become our 50th state, the Soviet Union no longer exists, China is a world power, and another attack on America is now the one most remembered. Today, the world is more than ever connected through the super highway of communication called the Internet. It is a different day for us, our children, and our grandchildren and it will continue to change. But as time ticks by, we owe it to those who served and those who died, to tell the story to the next generation of this part of history—"Let us not forget."

In memory of James Earl Smith

December 23, 1920 – June 10, 2011

BIBLIOGRAPHY

Combs, Sara. "Pearl Harbor Survivor Jim Smith recalls day that lives in infamy." *Crawford County Democrat* 6 December, 1991, pg.1.

Cable, Lee. "Never Forgetting That Day." *Clarion News* "Style" 25 July, 2007, pgs.1,4.

Cable, Lee. "Pearl Harbor Warriors, Survivors." *Clarion News* "Style" 15 July, 2009, pg.1.

Hall, C. Ray. "The Survivors." *The Courier-Journal* "Scene" 7 December 1991, pgs.4-7.

"Battle of Rennell Island." Wikipedia: The Free Encyclopedia. Wikipedia Foundation, Inc. 22 July 2004. Web. 17 October 2011. http://en.wikipedia.org/wiki/Battle of Rennell Island

"Battle of Tassafaronga." Wikipedia: The Free Encyclopedia. Wikipedia Foundation, Inc. 22 July 2004. Web. 17 October 2011. http://en.wikipedia.org/wiki/Battle of Tassafaronga

"USS *Arizona*." Wikipedia: The Free Encyclopedia. Wikipedia Foundation, Inc. 22 July 2004. Web. 17 October 2011. http://en.wikipedia.org/wiki/USS *Arizona* (BB-39)

" Pearl Harbor." Wikipedia: The Free Encyclopedia. Wikipedia Foundation, Inc. 22 July 2004. Web. 17 October 2011. http://en.wikipedia.org/wiki/Pearl Harbor

"Attack on Pearl Harbor." Wikipedia: The Free Encyclopedia. Wikipedia Foundation, Inc. 22 July 2004. Web. 17 October 2011. http://en.wikipedia.org/wiki/Attack on Pearl Harbor

Smith, James Earl. Personal Interview. 1 February, 2009 to 1 March, 2011.

Delaney, Elisha. Personal Interview. 10 May, 2011.

Roggenkamp, E.K. Personal Interview. 10 May, 2011.

Edwards, Jim. Personal Interview. 30 January, 2012.